What people ar

7 ꟻECRETS of L

(Excerpt from some of the reviews received.
Full reviews can be found at www.mercysong.com)

"In *7 Secrets of Divine Mercy*, Vinny Flynn opens our hearts and minds to the awesome gift of God's mercy for each one of us. In it he writes, 'Everything in our lives becomes more meaningful, more powerful, more life-changing once we understand and embrace Divine Mercy.' Thanks to this book, readers are given a guide to do just that."

— **Most Reverend William E. Lori**
Archbishop of Baltimore

"My new favorite book! I was so blessed to read it. In this book, Vinny Flynn makes Divine Mercy something approachable even as he unpacks just how amazing it is. Your prayer life and your approach to God will be transformed and, like me, you'll be thanking God for the gift of this book."

— **Sarah Reinhard**
Author and Blogger, SnoringScholar.com

"Nobody is better at helping us rediscover familiar devotional practices than Vinny Flynn. He's helped millions of people renew their connection to the Eucharist, Confession, and worship, and now he's heralding a fresh appreciation for Divine Mercy. If you want to experience more of the Lord's mercy and radiate it to others, read this excellent book."

— **Brandon Vogt**
Author, *RETURN: How to Draw Your Child Back to the Church*

"If you have never read a book on the Divine Mercy devotion, here is the best one to begin with. And if you have read many, here is the best guide to a more profound grasp of the mysterious secrets underlying the stupendous Mercy of the divine Persons. Highly recommended."

— **Fr. Peter Damian Fehlner, S.T.D.**
Author, *St. Maximilian Kolbe: Martyr of Charity*

"*7 Secrets of Divine Mercy* is a treasure for the promotion of the Divine Mercy devotion in the world. I recommend this book to all."

— **Most Rev. Martin Igwe Uzo ıkwu**
Bishop of Minna, Nigeria

"Vinny Flynn's *7 Secrets of Divine Mercy* accomplishes something that even most of us priests frequently fail to do: he takes deep theological concepts and makes them easy to understand! Divine Mercy is the most important message of our times, and Vinny's book is one of the most important books on my bookshelf!"

— **Fr. Chris Alar, MIC**
Director, Marian Press, Author, *Divine Mercy 101*

"More than a decade before St. Faustina's canonization, Vinny Flynn was the scribe extraordinaire, working with Fr. George Kosicki, CSB, and the Marian Fathers in often-cramped quarters, burning the midnight oil, teaching the teachers, and spreading the message of Divine Mercy at a grassroots level. This book is truly the culmination of years of loving labor ... now made accessible to all."

— **Felix Carroll**
Author, *Loved, Lost, Found: 17 Divine Mercy Conversions*

"Vinny Flynn does not disappoint in this third book of his "7 Secrets" series. *7 Secrets of Divine Mercy* is profound, relevant, inspired and captivating. This book breathes the love of God. Highly recommended!"

— **Kathleen Beckman, L.H.S.**
Author, *God's Healing Mercy, 2015*

"After helping the Marian Fathers promote the Divine Mercy message and devotion for 20 years, I thought that I had a reasonably good understanding of God's mercy. I now see Divine Mercy in a new light. This is an amazing book, a 'tour de force' on Divine Mercy that can change your life, as it has mine."

— **David Came**
Author, *Pope Benedict's Divine Mercy Mandate*

"Vinny Flynn has written an invaluable guide for anyone wishing to understand ever more deeply the gift of Divine Mercy. This is an accessible and profound response to Pope Francis' call for a renewed proclamation of God's merciful love."

— **Most Rev. Michael F. Burbidge**
Bishop of Raleigh

"A long-time student of St. Faustina, Flynn unpacks the essential elements of Divine Mercy and how it applies to the world we live in today. This is really an important book, a must-read for both priests and lay people."

— **Patrick Novecosky**
Editor-In-Chief, *Legatus* Magazine

"Flynn insightfully explains the mercy of God as the umbrella over all of God's gifts: creation, salvation, the sacraments, every activity, ritual — our very lives."

— **Steve Ray**
CatholicConvert.com

"Vinny Flynn has risen to the occasion in *7 Secrets of Divine Mercy* by instructing us in the way of Divine Mercy and leading us to contemplate the fascinating mystery of mercy. One of the best books I have ever read!"

— **Donna-Marie Cooper O'Boyle**
EWTN TV Host, Author, *The Kiss of Jesus*

"Put your spiritual seat-belts on. …This book will give you incredible insight into what all of us need most — God's great 'Mercy!'"

— **Terry Barber**
Author, *How to Share Your Faith with Anyone*

"Vinny Flynn's insightful work reveals the richness and beauty of God's mercy to every reader. *7 Secrets of Divine Mercy* is an important book for every disciple of Jesus Christ."

— **Most Reverend James Conley**
Bishop of Lincoln, Nebraska

7 SECRETS of DIVINE MERCY

Vinny Flynn

MERCYSONG
STOCKBRIDGE, MASSACHUSETTS

PUBLISHED BY MERCYSONG, INC.
Stockbridge, Massachusetts
www.mercysong.com

IN COLLABORATION WITH IGNATIUS PRESS
San Francisco, California, USA

Scripture citations, unless otherwise noted are taken from the
Revised Standard Version Bible, Ignatius Edition copyright © 2006,
Division of Christian Education of the National Council of the
Churches of Christ in the United States of America. All rights reserved.

Excerpts from the English translation of the *Catechism of the Catholic
Church* for use in the United States of America Copyright © 1994,
United States Catholic Conference, Inc. — Libreria Editrice Vaticana.
Used with Permission.

Quotations from the Diary of Saint Faustina are taken from
DIARY, Saint Maria Faustina Kowalska: Divine Mercy in My Soul
© 1987 Marian Fathers of the Immaculate Conception of the BVM,
Stockbridge, MA 01263. All rights reserved. Used with permission.

Library of Congress Control Number: 2019914192

ISBN: 978-1-884479-57-1

7 Secrets logo: Riz Boncan Marsella

Cover Design: Mary Flannery

Cover Art: The Vilnius Image, courtesy of
The Marians of the Immaculate Conception, Stockbridge, MA 01263.
This is the "original" version of the Divine Mercy Image,
painted in 1934 by Eugene Kazimierowski under the supervision
of St. Faustina and her confessor, Blessed Michael Sopocko, in Vilnius.
Copyright © 2011, Marians of the Immaculate Conception
Used with permission. All rights reserved.
Art prints are available through the Marians at
www.DivineMercyArt.com.

PRINTED IN THE UNITED STATES OF AMERICA

Second Edition
October, 2019

DEDICATION
IN MEMORIAM

To Fr. George W. Kosicki, C.S.B.
(July 29,1928 – August 11, 2014)

For whom Divine Mercy
was a Way of Life

Thank you, Father George!
May we all, like you, learn to
"Trust Even More!"

"The hour has come
to bring Christ's message
to everyone. …

The hour has come
when the message of Divine Mercy
is able to fill hearts with hope
and to become the spark
of a new civilization of love. …

How much the world needs
to understand and accept
Divine Mercy!"

Pope St. John Paul II

CONTENTS

Author's Note

Quotations used in the text are generally arranged by page number and section in the Notes, Sources, and References at the end. Quotations from Scripture, the *Catechism of the Catholic Church*, some Church documents, and the *Diary* of St. Faustina are cited in the text itself. Except for quotes from the *Catechism* and Scripture, all emphasis is the author's unless otherwise noted.

FOREWORD
Monopoly® Spirituality

*This people honors me with their lips,
but their hearts are far from me.*

Mt 15:8, NABRE

This is perhaps the book I should have written first. I wrote *7 Secrets of the Eucharist* and then *7 Secrets of Confession* because, as I traveled around the country giving talks at churches and conferences, I found that many people — perhaps most people — had a limited and often distorted view of these sacraments, and that a deeper awareness of what these sacraments are really all about could dramatically change their lives, as it has mine.

But, in a sense, I should have written about Divine Mercy first because everything depends on it. We can't really understand the sacraments — or anything else in the Church — until we understand Divine Mercy.

The Umbrella Devotion

All of creation is an act of mercy! Devotion to Divine Mercy is not just "a private devotion." It's *the* devotion, the "umbrella" devotion over everything else. Every other devotion in the Church, every ritual, every activity, every teaching is under that umbrella. It's all there to help us understand and enter into Divine Mercy.

Everything in our lives becomes more meaningful, more powerful, more life-changing once we understand and embrace Divine Mercy. It is the primary reality of our existence.

Once you start to see that, you notice mercy everywhere: in the Mass, in the Divine Office, in the

Catechism, in Scripture. "Oh, yeah, it's right here … and there, too … and here."

"Mercy is the very foundation of the Church's life," writes Pope Francis. "We need constantly to contemplate the mystery of mercy. … Our salvation depends on it":

> Mercy: the word reveals the very mystery of the Most Holy Trinity.
> Mercy: the ultimate and supreme act by which God comes to meet us.
> Mercy: the fundamental law that dwells in the heart of every person. …
> Mercy: the bridge that connects God and man.
>
> *Face of Mercy*, #10, 2

> This word changes everything. … It changes the world.
>
> *Angelus*, March 17, 2013

Saint Faustina

For many people in the Church today, "Divine Mercy" is synonymous with the Divine Mercy devotion based on the *Diary* of St. Faustina Kowalska, a

Polish nun, to whom, in the 1930s, the Lord revealed Himself as "The Divine Mercy."

The 600-page diary, which she entitled *Divine Mercy in My Soul*, recounts the story of remarkable revelations that Faustina received from the Lord — revelations that present a powerful *new focus on the Gospel message of mercy*, and that introduce various devotional elements and practices that have now become known throughout the world.

The **Divine Mercy Image** is displayed and revered in countless churches and homes; the **Chaplet of Divine Mercy** is prayed daily by millions of people; the three o'clock hour is observed as the **Hour of Great Mercy**; and the **Divine Mercy Novena** is solemnly prayed at many churches and shrines from Good Friday to the eve of the Second Sunday of Easter. That Sunday, in response to the Lord's request to Faustina, is now widely celebrated as the **Feast of Divine Mercy**.

In the year 2000, Pope John Paul II officially established the Feast as "Divine Mercy Sunday," and Faustina became the first saint of the Jubilee Year that ushered in the Third Millennium.

The "Problem" with Divine Mercy

Because the devotion to Divine Mercy has spread so quickly and has borne such wonderful fruit in people's lives — renewed peace and hope, remarkable conversions, miracles of grace, spiritual and physical healings — it has led some people to an almost superstitious focus on the devotional practices themselves.

Anything, even something good, can become an idol if it draws our focus *to itself* instead of to God. The Divine Mercy Image, for example, can be an icon — like a window leading us into a deeper relationship with God — or an idol, as if the painting itself has some kind of magic power.

The more graces we receive through particular prayers, rituals, and devotional practices, the easier it is to lose our focus on God and allow the medium to become the message. Gradually, our motivation can become, "What can I get from this devotion?"

Wow! This Image is so powerful! If I just hang it in my house, it will protect me and my family. If I pray the Chaplet every day, I'll get special grace. If I go to Confession and receive Communion on Mercy Sunday, I'll receive the great promise of forgiveness of sin and punishment.

Fr. George Kosicki, who wrote and taught extensively about Divine Mercy, used to illustrate this attitude by adapting the phrase "Go directly to Jail" from the game Monopoly®:

> Hang this picture on your wall, say this prayer, celebrate the Feast of Mercy, and go directly to Heaven without passing Go.

Devotion vs. Devotions

Are these devotional practices wrong? Is it wrong to hang the Image on my wall? Wrong to pray the Chaplet? Wrong to celebrate the Feast of Mercy?

Of course not! But we need to understand the real meaning and purpose of these outward practices, so that our *devotions* will lead us to deeper *devotion*.

Devotion means dedicating yourself, giving yourself completely to something or someone. In a religious context, it means completely dedicating yourself to God, belonging to Him, caring about Him and the things He cares about. It means allowing Him to touch your heart and give direction *to the way you live.*

Devotion to Divine Mercy involves a commitment to *live the message* of Divine Mercy. It's a decision to trust more and more in God, to accept His mercy with thanksgiving, and to be merciful as He is merciful.

Lip Service or Merciful Heart?

It comes down to some basic questions. Who do you want to be, a Pharisee or a disciple? The Pharisees practiced daily devotions. Lots of them. They did all the "right stuff." They said all the right prayers, performed all the proper rituals, fasted regularly, etc. But none of it touched their hearts. None of it led them into a deeper personal relationship with God so that they learned to live the way He wanted them to live.

There are two Scripture passages that help me to remember who I want to be, help me to refocus and rededicate myself to mercy in action:

1. This people honors me with their lips, but their hearts are far from me (Mt 15:8, NABRE).

2. Blessed are the merciful, for they shall obtain mercy (Mt 5:7).

If the Lord were to talk about you, which of these would you like to hear Him say? Does your heart lead you to live what your lips profess, or do you say one thing and do another like the hypocrites we see in the Gospel?

Pope Francis points out that, when Jesus was confronted by hypocrites, He was not deceived, for He knew their hearts. So, we should ask ourselves,

Can Jesus trust me, or am I two-faced? Do I play the Catholic … and then live as a pagan? … Jesus knows all that there is in our heart. We cannot deceive Jesus. In front of Him, we cannot pretend to be saints … and then live a life that is not what He wants. … If you do not live according to the spirit of the Beatitudes, you are not Catholic. You are a hypocrite.

Pope Francis, Homily, March 8, 2015

Pope St. John Paul II also spoke of this need to put mercy into practice, repeatedly emphasizing that Divine Mercy is, first of all, a way of life.

The "Demands" of Mercy

In one of his greatest encyclicals, Pope John Paul II wrote that Christ came to show us that God is a Father who is "rich in mercy." But he added,

> Christ, in revealing the love-mercy of God, at the same time *demanded from people* that they also should be guided *in their lives* by love and mercy.
>
> *Rich in Mercy*, #3

This need to put mercy into action has been Pope Francis' primary theme throughout his pontificate. Over and over again, he has urged the Church — and all of us individually — to come out of ourselves, dare to reach out beyond our comfort zones, and try to really live the Gospel message of mercy.

In April, 2015, he proclaimed an extraordinary Jubilee Year of Mercy and set as the motto for the year: *Merciful like the Father.* "How much I desire," he exclaimed, "that the year to come will be steeped in mercy, so that we can go out to every man and woman, bringing the goodness and tenderness of God!" (*Face of Mercy*, #5).

Time to Start Over

In his letter about the Jubilee Year, the Holy Father is inviting us to start over, to come to a renewed understanding and experience of the way we are loved by the Father, and then to commit ourselves to learning how to live out that same way of love in the world:

> The time has come for the Church to take up the joyful call to mercy once more. It is time to return to the basics and to bear the weaknesses and struggles of our brothers and sisters. ... This is the opportune moment to change our lives! This is the time to allow our hearts to be touched! ... [To] find the strength to embrace God's mercy and dedicate ourselves to being merciful with others as the Father has been with us.
>
> *Face of Mercy*, #10, 19, 14

In one of his homilies, Pope Francis used a phrase that has really stuck with me and that, for me, sums up what all of this is about. "We are called," he said, "to live lives *shaped by mercy*."

That's the purpose of this book: to invite you to take a deeper look at the message of Divine Mercy found in Scripture, the teachings of the Church, and the *Diary* of St. Faustina, so that you may respond more fully to the Lord's call to let your entire life be *"shaped by mercy."*

> Go forth! We are living in the age of mercy. This *is* the age of mercy.

> Pope Francis, *Angelus*, January 11, 2015

$\mathcal{S}$ECRET 1

God Has a Plan

*God has given us the wisdom to understand fully
the mystery, the plan He was pleased to decree ...*

Eph 1:9

I've written about "secrets" of the Eucharist and "secrets" of Confession, but to me, the greatest "secret" of all is that God has a plan.

When I mention this at the beginning of a talk, people give me some pretty strange looks, as if to say, "Well, duh, of course He has a plan! That's no secret! We all know that!"

And, in a way, they're right. If you believe in God as the Creator of the world, the idea that He has a plan probably isn't a startling revelation.

But, when was the last time you took that idea out and looked at it? Really thought about it?

So What?

My favorite question is "So what?" It's a question we often forget to ask. We simply accept some truth, some teaching, some statement and then move on, without ever really thinking about it.

God has a plan. So what? What exactly *is* His plan, and why did He decide on it? How does the world fit in with His plan? How does the Church fit in? How do all her rituals and teachings and sacraments relate to God's plan? (Because, if God doesn't have a plan, nothing in our faith makes sense.)

And how do you fit in? Why do you even exist? What about all the "stuff" of your daily life, at work, in your family, in your recreation? Does any of that relate? What's God's plan for *you?* Are you living "inside" His plan, or have you stepped "outside"? Are you actively participating in His plan, or are you oblivious to it, or perhaps even working against it?

I can say that I believe in God, that I'm a "practicing" Christian, that (like the Pharisees I mentioned in the Foreword) I say all the prescribed prayers and participate in the various traditions and rituals. But that's not enough if I don't think about *who* I am, *what* I'm doing, *why* I'm doing it, and *how it relates* to what God has in mind for me. As Socrates expressed it, "The unexamined life is not worth living."

So let's examine this plan of God.

What's It All About?

When he was a young man, Pope John Paul II wrote a poetic essay entitled "Reflections on Fatherhood," in which he expressed a central reality that sums up everything and that became the basis for all his later teachings. To me, it's a truth that we need to continually return to as we try to really understand God's plan.

"Everything else," he wrote, "will turn out to be unimportant and inessential except for this: …"

He then identified three things — only three.

Now think about your life, your family, your work, your desires, your hopes, your past, your present, your goals — all the things you think about, worry about, fret about, dream about each day.

According to Pope John Paul II, none of that will turn out to be important or necessary unless it relates to three things. In the whole history of the world, the whole universe, the whole story of this human adventure, only three things are important or necessary.

"Father, Child, Love"

Father, Child, Love. That's it. Anything else that you and I make important, anything else that you and I allow ourselves to get anxious about, to think about, to dwell on, to use energy upon — if it does not relate to these three things — is not important, not necessary.

In one sense, of course, we can interpret the Pope's words as referring to the Trinity: the Father, the Son, and the love that is between them, the Holy Spirit. As the Pope explained in one of his addresses, God Himself is the ultimate reality of *Father, Child, Love*:

God in his deepest mystery is not a solitude, but a *family*, since he has in himself *fatherhood*, *sonship*, and the essence of family, which is *love*.

What does this have to do with God's plan?

Everything. The Trinity is not just an idea, not just a theological concept. It's three *real* Persons in a Divine *Family* of love, and the Father's plan can only be understood in light of this Family.

I'm going to say that again: *The Father's plan can only be understood in light of this Family.*

The Plan of Mercy

The *Catechism of the Catholic Church* reveals that, before the world was created, God the Father had conceived a plan of mercy:

> Such is the "plan of his *loving kindness*," conceived by the *Father* before the foundation of the world in his beloved *Son*. "He destined us in love to be his sons" and "to be conformed to the image of his Son" through "the *Spirit* of Sonship" (Eph 1:4-5, 9; Rom 8:15, 29).
>
> #257; emphasis added

Wow! So *Father, Child, Love* isn't just about the Trinity. It's about the Trinity *and us*!

Before the creation of the world, God the *Father*, in His *Love*, planned for you and me to become His *children* — not just creatures, but *children*.

St. John speaks with awe about this reality:

> See what love the Father has given us that we should be called children of God; and so we are.
>
> 1 Jn 3:1

The Trinity — the mystery of mysteries, the greatest mystery in the Church — is all about love! It's all about Divine Love, given, received, and extended to all.

In the Trinity, God the Father is eternally loving the Son; the Son is eternally returning the love of the Father; and the Holy Spirit is the love between the Father and the Son!

In this endless cycle of self-giving love, the Son deserves the love of the Father, and the Father deserves the love of the Son. Who else deserves it? Nobody! Nobody else deserves it.

But true love longs to give of itself. So the Father decided to create more beings to love. In reality, that's what mercy is — when God, who is all-deserving, all-worthy, stoops to extend His love to mere creatures, who can't possibly deserve it.

Pope John Paul II, in his homily for the canonization of St. Faustina in 2000, explains that this extension of love, this "great wave of mercy" from the Father, comes to us through the pierced Heart of Jesus and is poured out upon us through the Holy Spirit. The entire Trinity is involved. *Mercy is the endless outflowing of Trinitarian love*:

> Divine Mercy reaches human beings through the Heart of Christ crucified. ... Christ pours out this mercy on humanity through the sending of the Spirit who, in the Trinity, is the Person-Love.
>
> Pope John Paul II, April 30, 2000

Creation itself is an expression of this outflowing love. You and I don't exist by accident, and we don't exist because God was bored. He wasn't just playing with clay:

> Hmmm … What shall I do to amuse Myself today? I think I'll just make up a batch of funny little creatures and watch what they do.

Silly image, isn't it? And so far removed from reality. We weren't created absent-mindedly by a disinterested God. We were created out of love. The *Catechism* tells us:

> "If man exists, it is because God has created him through love, and through love continues to hold him in existence" (Vat II, *GS* 19, par. 1).

#27

And St. Irenaeus adds:

> "In the beginning, God created Adam, not because he needed man, but because he *wanted to have someone on whom to bestow his blessings*."

But God didn't just want more *creatures* to bless. He wanted more *children* who could become part of the Family.

Whoa! Wait a minute! *Become part of the Trinity?* Yes. This will gradually become clearer as we go along.

> God . . does not merely remain closely linked to the world as the Creator. … He is also *Father*: … linked to man … by a bond still more intimate than that of creation. It is love which not only creates the good but also grants participation in the very life of God: Father, Son and Holy Spirit. For he who loves desires to give himself.
>
> *Rich in Mercy*, #7

This is so important to understand! We need to let this really sink in. You and I were not merely created; we were *fathered-forth* from the Heart of God. And we are *linked to the Father* by a bond of love that *grants us participation* in the life of the Trinity. The very first paragraph of the *Catechism* teaches us:

> God … in a plan of sheer goodness freely created man to make him *share in his own blessed life*. … To accomplish this, when the fullness of time had come, God sent his Son as Redeemer and Savior. In his Son and through him, he invites men to become, in the Holy Spirit, his *adopted children* and thus *heirs of his blessed life*.
>
> #1; emphasis added

Christ was sent to redeem and save us to fulfill the Father's plan of mercy — that we would become His *adopted children* and *inherit His blessed life.*

What does that really mean?

Another passage in the *Catechism* gives us the beginning of a very specific answer:

> The Father's power "raised up" Christ his Son and by doing so perfectly introduced his Son's humanity, including his body, into the Trinity.

#648

The God-Man

Okay. To understand this, we need to look briefly at another mystery: the Incarnation.

Jesus Christ always existed, right?

Wrong. "In the beginning was the Word" (Jn 1:1). The Word — the Second Person of the Trinity — always existed, "begotten, not made, consubstantial with the Father" (Nicene Creed). Then, "when *the fullness of time had come*, God sent his Son, born of a woman ..." (Gal 4:4, NRSV; emphasis added).

At this precise moment in time, the Divine Son of the Father assumed a human nature — including a fully human body — from the Virgin Mary. As we proclaim at every Mass, He "came down from Heaven, and by the Holy Spirit was incarnate of the Virgin Mary, and became man" (Nicene Creed).

Incarnate. He took on flesh from Mary. Existing from all eternity as God, He now, at Mary's "yes," becomes the God-Man: still fully divine, but now also fully human. And He receives the name that Mary was told to give Him: "You will conceive in your womb and bear a son, and you shall name him Jesus" (Lk 1:31, NABRE).

As the *Catechism* explains:

> "He was begotten from the Father before all ages *as to his divinity* and in these last days, for us and for our salvation, was born *as to his humanity* of the virgin Mary, the Mother of God."
>
> #467; emphasis added

Now let's go back to that earlier quote from

the *Catechism:* "The Father's power 'raised up' Christ his Son …"

Wait a minute! Why did Christ need to be raised up? He's God, isn't He?

Yes. His divinity was not subject to death, and so needed no raising up. And His divine nature was never separated from the Trinity. The Trinity cannot be split up. The Father, the Son, and the Spirit are one — they cannot be divided.

But in His *humanity*, Jesus was just like you and me in every way except sin — with a human body and a human soul. In His humanity, He suffered and died on the Cross, and His lacerated body was buried. So the Father, by His divine power, raised Him from the dead.

Now look again at the rest of the quote:

> and by doing so perfectly introduced his Son's humanity, *including his body*, into the Trinity.
>
> #648; emphasis added

I find it really interesting that the *Catechism* is so precise here. It doesn't just say the Father introduced

Christ's humanity into the Trinity; it adds "including His body." Christ's entire human nature, including His body, was introduced by the Father into the Trinity itself.

And what's His body like? Was Christ raised from the dead just like Lazarus or Jairus' daughter? Back to life as usual? No. The Church teaches that

> Christ's Resurrection was not a return to earthly life. … In his risen body he passes from the state of death to *another life beyond time and space*. … his body is filled with the power of the Holy Spirit: he *shares the divine life*.
>
> *Catechism*, #646; emphasis added

Divinization

So what? Why am I going on about this? Because everything the Father did for Jesus, He wants to do for you and me.

You and I are destined by God, if we cooperate, to be *introduced by the Father into the Trinity*. That's what God wants for you and me. His wish, His desire, His thirst is to be able, someday, to lovingly, perfectly introduce each one of us, in our now glorified bodies, into the Trinity itself, where we will *share the divine life*. That's Heaven. That's what we are called to. *That's God's plan.*

This is so clear in Scripture and the teaching of the Church. At each Mass we pray that we may "come *to share in the divinity of Christ*, who humbled himself to share in our humanity." St. Peter tells us that the Word became flesh to make us *"partakers of the divine nature"* (2 Pet 1:4; emphasis added). And, in *Lumen Gentium*, we read that "the eternal Father ... chose to raise up men *to share in his own divine life*" (#2).

The *Catechism* teaches that we are all "called to share in the life of the Blessed Trinity" (#265), and that our adoption as children of God "gains us a real share in the life of the only Son" (#654). And it gets even more specific, quoting first St. Athanasius:

> By the participation of the Spirit, we become communicants in the divine nature. ... For this reason, those in whom the Spirit dwells are *divinized*. ... "The Son of God

became man *so that we might become God.*"

#1988, 460; emphasis added

And then St. Thomas Aquinas:

> "The only-begotten Son of God, want-ing to make us sharers in his divinity, assumed our nature, so that he, made man, might make men gods."

#460

Some people get really upset about this: "Hey, wait a minute, I can't become God!"

No, not if that means being equal to God, taking over for God, replacing God. But we are called to such a complete union with God, such an intimate sharing of His divine nature, His way of living, that we can one day say with St. Paul, "It is no longer I who live, but Christ who lives in me" (Gal 2:20).

In the plan of God, we were not created to remain merely human; we were created to become *divinely* human, just like Christ — to pass from death to *another life beyond time and space* — a life in the Trinity Itself.

Another life. After we die, we pass to another life. Well, of course! We know that. Christians have always believed in life after death. We live here for a while, then we die, and then we live again forever — eternal life, right?

Wrong. Eternal life doesn't mean that we just live again forever. It's *another kind of life*, a whole *new way of living*. It's when we live with and in the Trinity, sharing the way God Himself lives. (And it can actually start now — but more about that later.)

Pope Benedict XVI, in his book, *God Is Near Us*, writes:

> Eternity is not just endless time, but another level of being. ... Eternal life is not simply what comes afterward. ... It is a *new quality of existence.*

So we've seen that, in the Father's plan of mercy, we were created out of love and destined to be introduced into the eternal life of the Trinity, called to be part of the Family of God. This is the plan that Christ came into the world to fulfill: "For God so loved the world, that He gave His only-begotten Son, that whoever believes in Him shall not perish, but have eternal life" (Jn 3:16, NASB).

Not Just Created, but Chosen

But we also need to understand that this plan is not just a general plan for the world; it's a very specific, personal plan for you.

Years ago, at a Divine Mercy conference, I heard a talk by one of the other speakers that changed everything for me. It was given by Babsie Bleasdell, a wonderful, holy woman and a well-known speaker from Trinidad.

Her opener got everyone's attention:

> I don't know many of you personally, but
> I know something about your mothers.

Some of us on the team looked at each other as if to say, "Hmm, where is she going with *this?*"

"Your mother had a million eggs." And she went on to explain that, because of the number of eggs present in a woman's body and the number of sperm cells generated in a man's body, each with its own, unique DNA (it's all there; it's built in), there are, at the very least, millions of human persons who could come from the union of a man and a woman.

She turned then to Fr. Hal Cohen, who was on the team with us, and she asked, "Fr. Hal, you're an only child, aren't you?" And he replied, "Why yes, Babsie, I am." She laughed and said, "You are one in a million!"

I laughed with everyone else, but the teaching that followed gave me a whole new insight into Divine Mercy and my own relationship with the "Father of mercies" (2 Cor 1:3).

What she explained is that a man and a woman don't have the ability to choose which child, of all those millions of possibilities, will actually be conceived. But God does.

The image that comes to mind is of a young married couple walking into a doctor's office and being shown into a large viewing room with a wall-sized movie screen. The doctor gives them a clicker, and they happily surf through pictures and personality charts for all the possible children they could have.

Oh, I like the tall, blonde one! ... or maybe the one with the green eyes and the nice smile ... but this one is so artistic ... but look at that one; he might become a great scientist.

All the DNA is already there, right? So if they could project all the possibilities, they could choose exactly which child they want to give life to.

Sadly, there are people (including some well-intentioned people) who, confused and deceived by worldly values, frustrated by unfortunate situations, or caught in the clutches of their own wants and needs, are trying to "play God" in this area.

Many couples, in their planning to have children, or in their discovery that a life has already begun through them, feel that they have the right to choose the gender or other genetic traits of the child to be born or to decide whether a child already conceived should be allowed to continue living.

None of us have that right, nor can we look into the future to know what the ramifications of our choices will be.

But God *can* and *does*. Only God has the right to make such a choice, and only God can project all the possibilities. He sees the whole picture, the whole story — and He sees through the eyes of love, not self-focused desires. God knows all "possibles." He knows past, present, and future all at once; He sees it all. He also sees all that *could have* happened, and all that *could happen* in the future. He sees everything, and He sees it all with mercy.

So what?

So you were not just *created*; you were *seen* and *chosen*. From all the millions of human persons who could have come from the union of your father and mother, God picked *you*.

There's a wonderful phrase in the Book of Jeremiah:

> Before I formed you in the womb I knew you.

Jer 1:5

Think about that! This is *God*, talking to *you:* "Before I formed you in the womb I knew you." And when God *knows*, He *loves*.

How and when did God know each of us? It's all in Psalm 139 (NIV):

> O LORD, you have searched me and you know me. You know when I sit and when I rise; you perceive my thoughts from afar. ...
>
> Before a word is on my tongue, you know it completely, O LORD. ...
>
> For you created my inmost being; you knit me together in my mother's womb. ...
>
> My frame was not hidden from you when I was made in the secret place.
>
> When I was woven together in the depths of the earth, your eyes saw my unformed body. All the days ordained for me were written in your book before one of them came to be.

In the *Diary* of St. Faustina, there's a beautiful conversation between Jesus and Faustina that speaks of this same reality:

> When I received Holy Communion, I said to Him, "Jesus, I thought about You so many times last night," and Jesus answered me, **And I thought of you before I called you into being. ... Before I made the world,**

I loved you with the love your heart is experiencing today and, throughout the centuries, My love will never change.

Diary, 1292, 1754

God "thought" of you before you were born. And, as Pope Francis says, "God always *thinks with mercy*" (Audience, March 27, 2013).

Not Just All, but Each

Pope Benedict XVI, in his first homily as pope, stressed that the human race didn't just "evolve," but that *each* of us was *thought into being* by God:

> We are not some casual and meaningless product of evolution. Each of us is the result of a *thought of God*. Each of us is *willed*, each of us is *loved*, each of us is *necessary*.

You exist because God *thought* of you. He knew everything about you. He knew everything you would ever do, all your physical characteristics, emotional characteristics, mental characteristics, everything; and of all the millions who could have been given life through your mother and father, He picked *you!* That's amazing! That's the dignity of each human person.

And that's why abortion is always wrong, even in cases of rape or incest. No matter how tragic, how violent, how awful the circumstances brought about by sin, the reality is that God knows each person who could come from that union, and chooses the one He wants born — and promises to love that child forever.

Pope John Paul II spent his whole pontificate trying to teach us about the dignity of each human person. In his homily at the canonization of St. Faustina on April 30, 2000, he said:

> The message of divine mercy is also implicitly a message about the value of every human being. *Each* person is precious in God's eyes; Christ gave his life for *each* one; to *everyone* the Father gives his Spirit and offers intimacy.

God didn't just love the *world*; He loved *you*. Christ didn't just suffer and die for *humanity*; He suffered and died for *you, personally*. Christ on the Cross was Man, but He was also God. He not only knew you and loved you from the Cross, but knew and loved you *during His whole life:*

> Jesus knew and loved us *each* and *all* during his life, his agony, and his Passion and gave himself up for *each one* of us.
>
> *Catechism,* #478; emphasis added

What an awesome reality! God knew everything about me before He created me, and He wanted me to live anyway! Christ saw me from the Cross and died to save me. For much of my life I never knew that. I never realized how special we each are to God. I mean, how could I be worried about anything? How could I not trust in this God who knew everything about me and thought me into being, this Father, who sent His Son to suffer and die for me?

Years ago, when I was preparing a talk about how personally each of us is chosen and loved by God, I put together a selection of quotes from Scripture that I call, "The Father's Love Letter to His Children."

As you read it, try to imagine God the Father saying all this personally to you:

Fear not, for I have redeemed you; I have called you by name, you are mine (Is 43:1). ... Before I formed you in the womb I knew you (Jer 1:5). ... See, upon the palms of my hands I have written your name (Is 49:16, NAB). ... I have loved you with an everlasting love (Jer 31:3). ... You are precious in my eyes (Is 43:4). ... Even the hairs of your head are all numbered (Mt 10:30).

Can a mother forget her infant, be without tenderness for the child of her womb? Even should she forget, I will never forget you (Is 49:15, NABRE). ... Though the mountains leave their place and the hills be shaken, My love will never leave you (Is 54:10, NAB). ... I will be a father to you, and you shall be my sons and daughters (2 Cor 6:18).

For I know well the plans I have in mind for you, ... plans for your welfare, not for woe! plans to give you a future full of hope. When you call me, when you go to pray to me, I will listen to you. ... When you seek me with all your heart, you will find me with you (Jer 29:11-14, NAB).

This is how important you are to God, how tenderly and personally He loves you, how deeply He longs to fulfill His plan to introduce you into the Trinity, to welcome you into His Family.

One in Christ

Okay, there's just one *final dimension* of God's plan that we need to look at. This is, in a very real sense, the culmination of everything we've seen so far.

I'm convinced that our greatest need is to understand — to really know — how loved we are by God, not just a "head knowledge," but a "heart knowledge" as well. I need to know and accept with all my being that God is my real Father, that He wanted me to be born, that He chose me, that He loves me differently than He has ever loved anyone else, and that His plan for me is to be with Him forever.

And then I need to understand that the same is true for you — and for each of His other children. We are each God's "favorite kid." He loves each of us in a completely unique, one-on-one way. And, like any good father, His greatest desire is that we will love each other the same way He loves us. His greatest desire is that we will all be one in Him.

That's the final dimension of His plan to introduce us into the Trinity with Him. St. Paul, in his Letter to the Ephesians, explains this final dimension:

> God has given us the wisdom to understand fully the mystery, the plan he was pleased to decree in Christ, a plan to be carried out in Christ, in the fullness of time, to bring all things into one in him in the heavens and on the earth.
>
> Eph 1:3-4, 9-10

This plan is to be *carried out in Christ*. Notice, it doesn't say *by* Christ but *in* Christ. This will become clearer later.

What does St. Paul identify as the ultimate purpose of this plan? *To bring all things into one in Him.* A familiar phrase to most Christians. But what does it really mean? Let's let Christ teach us, as He taught the disciples at the Last Supper.

The scene is the Cenacle, the Upper Room, where so much took place. The Passover meal has ended,

Judas has left to betray the Lord, and Jesus is giving His last discourse to the disciples, just before entering into His Passion in the Garden of Gethsemane.

He begins by giving them something new:

> A new commandment I give to you, that you love one another; even as I have loved you, that you also love one another.
>
> Jn 13:34

Then, to help us understand what He means, He gives us a glimpse of the way He loves and is loved in the Trinity — a union of love so close, so complete that it involves an *indwelling*, whereby each Person lives *in* the other.

He starts to talk to the disciples about the Father, and Philip interrupts Him, asking, "Lord, *show* us the Father." Jesus responds:

> He who has seen me, has *seen* the Father; how can you say, "*Show* us the Father"? Do you not believe that I am *in* the Father and the Father is *in* me? The words that I say to you I do not speak on my own authority; but the Father who *dwells in me*

does His works. Believe me that I am *in* the
Father and the Father is *in* me.

> Jn 14:8-11; emphasis added

He goes on to make it clear that we, too, are
involved in this union of love through the dwelling of
the three Persons *in us* and us *in them*. He tells the disciples that He will ask the Father to send them the
Holy Spirit, explaining that the Spirit "dwells with
you, and will be in you" (Jn 14:17). And He continues:

> I am *in* my Father, and you *in* me, and I
> *in* you. ... He who loves me will be loved by
> my Father ... and *we* will come to him and
> *make our home* with him.
>
> Jn 14:20-21, 23; emphasis added

The High Priestly Prayer

At the end of His instruction to the disciples, the
Lord then begins praying aloud to the Father in their
presence. This is the "High Priestly Prayer of Jesus,"
the "Prayer of Unity." It's the longest prayer recorded
in the Gospels, and, to me, the most passionate. In

this prayer Christ reveals his greatest desire for you and me, a desire so important to Him that He pleads with the Father for it, not once, but four times:

> Father, ... *that they may be one*, even as we are one. ...

> I do not pray for these only [the disciples], but also for those who believe in me through their word [you and me], *that they may all be one;* even as you, Father, are in me, and I in you, that they may also be in us.

> *that they may be one* even as we are one, I in them and you in me, *that they may become perfectly one.*
>
> Jn 17:11, 20-23; emphasis added

Please don't just read that and then move on. Let's sit with this a bit and try to understand what's really happening in this Gospel scene.

Christ knows that His hour has come. He knows that Judas has left the Cenacle to betray Him. He knows that, as soon as He finishes speaking to the disciples, it will be time to go to Gethsemane to take on the greatest sufferings imaginable.

At this critical moment, what is He thinking about? His agony and death? No. He's thinking about you and me, and He's praying aloud to the Father so you and I will hear and understand that, to Him, we are worth dying for.

The plan of mercy, the "*plan born in the Father's Heart*" (*Catechism*, #759) from all eternity, has now, in the fullness of time, taken root in the Heart of Christ so completely that He's willing to suffer and die to accomplish that plan. The greatest wish of the Father is the greatest wish of the Son — *that you and I may become one in Them.*

We Need to Really "Get" the Plan

It's been a pretty long chapter, and I've thrown a lot of stuff at you, and I want to make sure that it doesn't just become an information overload. So let me just try to tie the pieces together because, before we go any further, it's important to really get what this is all about.

The ultimate reality is *Father, Child, Love*, and this reality is eternally expressed in the Trinity, the Family from which all other families draw their source.

God the Father is eternally *Father*. That's not just His title. It's *His whole being*. He does not exist apart from His fathering, does not exist apart from His loving relationship with His Son.

The Son is eternally the *Son*. He does not exist apart from His sonship, does not exist apart from His loving relationship with His Father.

The Holy Spirit is eternally the *Love* of the Father and the Son. He does not exist apart from that Love. He *is* that Love in Person.

> "The Father is wholly in the Son and wholly in the Holy Spirit; the Son is wholly in the Father and wholly in the Holy Spirit; the Holy Spirit is wholly in the Father and wholly in the Son."
>
> *Catechism*, #255

The Trinity is a totally united Family of never-ending, self-giving, interpersonal Love. And you and I exist because God the Father wants us to join the Family. That's His plan.

Before the world began, God saw you, knew you, loved you, chose you, and then fathered you forth, thinking you into being as He lovingly formed you in your mother's womb. And he did the same for me.

Is it any wonder, then, that Christ's greatest desire is for us to be one with each other, united in reciprocal love? Only when we have learned to live in His love and to love one another as He has loved us can the Father's plan of mercy be realized.

$\mathscr{S}$ECRET 2
Good Enough Isn't Good Enough

> **To be a saint is not a luxury.**
> **It is necessary.**
>
> *Pope Francis*

In Secret 1, we saw the "good news" of God's plan of mercy, the amazing reality that God the Father wants each of us to enter into the Trinity Itself to be with Him forever.

Now here's the "bad news."

Nothing unholy can enter the holiness of God. Period. End of sentence.

I never knew that. I knew that the saints were holy, but I never remember anyone even suggesting that *everyone* had to be holy, that *I*, myself, had to become holy. I admired the saints and, at some level, felt inspired to be a better person; but it had never really clicked with me that I was supposed to be one of them. They were special people, set apart by God.

For me, good enough was good enough. I went to church, tried to keep the rules, and tried to be a good person, but the idea of me actually becoming a saint wasn't even on my radar.

Thy Kingdom Come

Eventually, as an adult, I started learning about the universal call to holiness (see *Catechism*, #2013) that has always been a part of Church teaching: the reality that God wants each of us to be holy — and that it's not optional; it's a requirement.

St. Paul makes this pretty clear:

> Strive for peace with everyone, and *for that holiness without which no one will see the Lord* (Heb 12:14, NAB; emphasis added).

> This is the will of God, your holiness: that you refrain from immorality ... for God does not call us to impurity but to holiness (1 Thes 4:3, 7, NAB).

> Be sure of this, that no immoral or impure or greedy person ... has any inheritance in the kingdom of Christ (Eph 5:5, NAB).

> Put to death, therefore, whatever belongs to your earthly nature: sexual immorality, impurity, lust, evil desires, and greed, which is idolatry (Col 3:5, NIV).

If we want to see God, if we want to be heirs of the kingdom, living with Christ in the Trinity, this is what is required. The Trinity is not a dysfunctional Family, where some of the members don't get along with each other. To live in the Family of God, we need to be *like* God. We need to be holy as He is holy. Holiness is the prerequisite for entering Heaven.

St. Paul gets even more specific:

> Live by the Spirit, I say, and do not gratify the desires of the flesh. ... Now the works of the flesh are obvious ...
>
> Gal 5:16, 19, NRSV

I always have to pause and chuckle a bit at this point. St. Paul begins by telling us that the works of the flesh are obvious, and then — just in case they're not obvious to *us* — he lists them:

> fornication, impurity, licentiousness, idolatry, sorcery, enmities, strife, jealousy, anger, quarrels, dissensions, factions, envy, drunkenness, carousing, and things like these.
>
> I am warning you, as I warned you before: those who do such things will not inherit the kingdom of God.
>
> By contrast, the fruit of the Spirit is love, joy, peace, patience, kindness, generosity, faithfulness, gentleness, and self-control.
>
> Gal 5:19-23, NRSV

So, according to St. Paul, if we want to *inherit the kingdom,* we need to be holy. Christ, Himself, tells us: "Unless your righteousness exceeds that of the scribes and Pharisees, you will never enter the kingdom of heaven" (Mt 5:20).

And we are given three scriptural commands that let us know exactly *how holy* God expects us to be. Are you sitting down? He has set the bar extremely high:

> Be holy; for I, the LORD, your God, am
> holy.
>
> Lev 20:7, NAB

> Be perfect, as your heavenly Father is
> perfect.
>
> Mt 5:48, NAB

> Be merciful, as your Father is merciful.
>
> Lk 6:36

God expects — and demands — that you and I become holy because *He* is holy. What does this holiness consist of? Being perfect *as He* is perfect. How is this perfection to be expressed? By being merciful *as He* is merciful.

That's a pretty tall order. God has given us a three-fold command that seems impossible to fulfill. He expects us to be holy *just like Him.*

The Paradox of Holiness

But there's a paradox here. What's a paradox? It's an apparent contradiction. It's when two statements seem absurd or contradictory, but actually express a truth. (G.K. Chesterton defined paradox as "truth standing on her head to attract attention.")

Scripture, as we've seen, tells us repeatedly that we have to be holy in the same way God is holy; but we also read in Scripture:

> There is none holy like the LORD.
>
> 1 Sam 2:2

> Who will not fear you, Lord, or glorify your name? For you alone are holy.
>
> Rev 15:4, NABRE

We find the same paradox in Church teaching and the Liturgy. The *Catechism* tells us:

> "All Christians in any state or walk of life are called to the fullness of Christian life and to the perfection of charity." All are called to holiness.
>
> #2013

But, during each Sunday Mass, we proclaim in the Gloria:

> For *you alone are the Holy One*, You alone are the Lord, You alone are the Most High, Jesus Christ.
>
> *Roman Missal*, 8

So how do we reconcile this apparent contradiction? If only God is holy, how can He demand that *we* be holy?

Think back to all that we saw about God's plan. The Father plans to introduce each of us into the Trinity. We are called to become *divinely human*, to *share the divine life*, to live in Christ and He in us.

Wholly One with the Holy One

The holiness that is demanded of us is *not our own holiness*; it's the *holiness of God in us* through the indwelling of His Holy Spirit. We can't come to holiness on our own. The only way we can become holy is by sharing God's holiness.

If you'll pardon a little play on words, we become *holy* to the extent that we are *wholly* incorporated into Christ. He alone is the *Holy One*.

We become holy when we are *wholly one* with Him, allowing *His* holiness to dwell in us and to shape our lives so completely that we begin to live and love the way He does, reflecting and expressing His holiness, His mercy.

To Pope Francis, it's like the sun and the moon:

> We Christians identify Christ with the sun, and the moon with the Church, the community of the faithful. The moon *does not have its own light*, and if the moon is hidden from the sun, it becomes dark. The sun is Jesus Christ. ... *No one, save Jesus Christ, possesses his or her own light.* ... May each of us be a *true reflection of his light and his love*.
>
> Ecuador, July 5, 2015

We have no light of our own, no holiness of our own. But we are each called to be like the full moon, shining brightly with the light of the Son. We are each called to reflect in our daily lives the holiness of the One who is the source of all holiness.

Okay, so here's the deal. God wants to bring us into the Trinity with Him. But that can't happen until we're holy, because we can't live *with* Him until we're *like* Him.

So, how do we get there? I don't know about you, but I've tried to make myself holy, and I can't do it. I often find myself complaining with St. Paul,

> I have the desire to do what is good, but I cannot carry it out. For I do not do the good I want to do, but the evil I do not want to do.
>
> Rom 7:18-19, NIV

So, what's the problem? Couldn't God have made it a little easier? If He wanted us to be holy, couldn't He have just made us that way to begin with?

A Creative Plan

He did. At least in the sense that He created us in such a way that we could *become* holy. *The problem is sin.* Let's take a look at creation in God's plan.

From the time I was a young kid dutifully going to Sunday school, if someone had asked me how God created us, I could proudly answer, "In His image and likeness." Like most Catholic kids at the time, I had obediently memorized various passages from the *Baltimore Catechism*.

But it was years later that I finally asked my favorite question:

> So what? What does it really mean that

we were created in His image and likeness?
And why did He create us that way?

I find it interesting that the creation account in Genesis (1:26-27; emphasis added) is very precise and seems a bit redundant. First we're told:

> God said, "Let us make man in *our image*, after *our* likeness."

On one level, we might interpret this as God the Father using the "royal we," but we can also see it as an emphasis that the whole Trinity is involved in this "image and likeness" creation.

The story goes on:

> So God created man in his *own* image,

And then, in case we're not really getting the point about what *his own image* is, we're told the same thing again with slightly different wording:

> in the image of *God* he created him.

What's being emphasized in this seemingly unnecessary repetition? *Divinity*. We were created to resemble the three divine Persons of the Trinity.

Let's go a little deeper. In its teaching about Christ's *body* when the "Word became flesh," the *Catechism* explains that, "In the body of Jesus, we see our *God made visible*. ... The individual characteristics of Christ's *body* express the *divine person* of God's Son" (#477; emphasis added).

So all the *individual characteristics* of Christ's *human* body reveal and express His *divinity*.

But that's only true of Christ's body, right? Only because He's God?

No. Christ, in His humanity, was "like us in all things but sin" (*Catechism* #467), so it's true of your body, too:

> "God fashioned man with his own hands
> ... and impressed *his own form* on the flesh
> he had fashioned, in such a way that *even
> what was visible might bear the divine form*."
>
> *Catechism*, #704; emphasis added

So what does all this tell us? That God, in order to be able to some day fulfill His plan (to introduce us into the Trinity to share in His divine way of living), created us to be so completely like Him that even our physical bodies could reflect and express His divinity, His *holiness*. (We'll see more about this in Secret 7).

And then came sin. Here we are, with even our bodies reflecting the divine beauty and holiness of God, and *Pow!* We're disfigured by sin.

> Disfigured by sin and death, man remains "in the image of God," in the image of the Son, but is deprived "of the glory of God," of his *"likeness."*
>
> *Catechism*, # 705; emphasis added

Suddenly, we're not *like* God anymore. We're still in His image, but that image in us is now disfigured, because its likeness to God has been lost. We don't *look* like Him, we don't *think* like Him, we don't *act* like Him, we don't *love* like Him. So God says:

> Okay, so much for *that* plan! They blew it. I'll just have to throw this batch away and start over with some better clay.

Silly, huh? But He could have done that, right? After all, He's God. He could have scrapped His plan for us and created some other beings.

Graceful Entry

But He didn't. Why? Because He loves us. Forever. No matter what. Having created us in Christ, the Father now sends Christ to re-create us, to restore us in the divine likeness:

> The Son himself will assume that "image" and restore it in the Father's "likeness" by giving it again its Glory, the Spirit who is "the giver of life."
>
> *Catechism*, #705

> It is in Christ, "the image of the invisible God," that man has been created "in the image and likeness" of the Creator. It is in Christ, Redeemer and Savior, that the divine image, disfigured in man by the first sin, has been restored to its original beauty and ennobled by the grace of God.
>
> *Catechism*, #1701

> His grace restores what sin had damaged in us.
>
> *Catechism*, #1708

His *grace* restores. *Grace* — a familiar word to most Christians. But what does it mean? And how does it restore?

I always thought I knew what grace was. To me it was a kind of help that God gives us when we ask for it. And I asked for it a lot:

> Lord, give me the grace to do well on this test. ... Give me the grace to overcome this bad habit. ... Give my son the grace of deeper conversion. ... Give me the grace to endure this pain ... etc.

Is grace really some kind of help that God gives us? Yes. But it's so much more! And it's all about how we enter into the holiness we're called to.

The *Catechism* begins it's discussion of grace by telling us that it's "the *free and undeserved* help that God gives us" (#1996).

Okay, so far so good. I guess I was right all those years. Grace is just help. Not quite! It's help that God gives us for *a specific purpose*: "to respond to his call to become children of God, adoptive sons, partakers of the divine nature and of eternal life" (#1996).

What's this really come down to?

> Grace is a *participation in the life of God.*
> It introduces us into the intimacy of
> Trinitarian life.
>
> *Catechism*, #1997

Is this starting to sound familiar, like an echo of something we've already seen? *Introduces* us? Into the life of the *Trinity?* That's why you and I were created, remember? God the Father wants to introduce each of us into the Trinity.

And there's still more:

> The grace of Christ is the gratuitous gift
> that God makes to us *of his own life*, infused
> by the Holy Spirit into our soul to heal it of
> sin and *to sanctify it.*
>
> *Catechism*, #1999; emphasis added

What does *sanctify* mean? To make holy. Grace is Christ's own life, His own holiness, poured into us to heal us of sin, restore us as children of God, and make us holy, so that the Father can fulfill His plan of mercy and bring us into the Trinity with Him.

He does this especially through the sacraments.

As I write this, a phrase I memorized as a kid from the old *Baltimore Catechism* jumps out at me: "A sacrament is an outward sign, instituted by Christ to give grace."

The purpose of the sacraments is to *give us grace, to heal us and make us holy* so that we can become like God and ultimately be with Him forever.

Through the sacraments, Christ re-creates us, restoring our disfigured nature so we can resemble Him again — "so that in him we might become the very righteousness of God" (2 Cor 5:21).

Long for Holiness

When I learned this, I asked my spiritual director what I could do to hasten this process, what I could do to become holy. He said, "Long for it, and be patient. The more you continue longing for it, the more you increase your capacity to receive it."

I found the same directive in the writings and talks of Pope John Paul II, who said that what the world needs is a "*true longing for holiness*" (*As the Third*

Millennium Draws Near, #42; emphasis original). Over and over again, wherever he went, he challenged his listeners, young and old, not to be afraid to be saints, not to be afraid of holiness, but to long for holiness, to strive for holiness, to dare to be saints.

This striving for holiness, he explained, involves four specific things: conversion, personal renewal, intense prayer, and solidarity with our neighbor.

When I read that, it was like a wake-up call. Wow! He's talking to me! I'm called to be holy. And if I want that to happen, I need to long for it, and I need to work at it. I need to work on *me*. I have to convert *me*. *I* have to be renewed. *I* have to pray intensely. *Solidarity* with my neighbor? I have to *care about other people*.

So now, when anyone asks me if I have any intentions that I could use prayer for, I say, "Yes: *holiness*." In the words of one of my favorite worship songs,

> Holiness is what I long for
> Holiness is what I need.

Micah Stampley

$\mathscr{S}$ECRET 3

It's Not Just a Picture of Jesus

> **Mercy has become living
> and visible in Jesus.**
>
> Pope Francis

Like many people, when I think of Divine Mercy, the image that immediately comes to mind (yes, another shameless pun), is the Divine Mercy Image, the picture of the Lord as He appeared to St. Faustina in 1931.

More than anything else, it is this Image that has drawn people to explore and embrace the message of Divine Mercy found in Faustina's *Diary*. It's the central feature of the *Diary* and, to those who look deeply, it reveals the entire story of mercy. It is a summary of the whole Paschal mystery (the Passion, Death, Resurrection, and Ascension); the whole Gospel; the whole *Catechism*; the whole plan of mercy.

Faustina's *Diary* begins with a reference to the Lord's command that she paint an image of Him:

> O Eternal Love, You command Your Sacred Image to be painted and reveal to us the inconceivable fount of mercy ...
>
> *Diary*, 1

It may be that my memory is failing me (they say it's the first thing to go) or that there are simply events that I'm not aware of, but I don't recall any other time in the history of our Lord's revelations to His people in which He directly asked anyone to paint a picture of Him.

His words to St. Faustina were very specific:

> **Paint an image according to the pattern you see ... .**
>
> *Diary*, 47

Not sure of what to do, Faustina mentioned this to her confessor. She writes:

> When I told this to my confessor, I received this for a reply: "That refers to your soul." He told me, "Certainly, paint God's image in your soul." When I came out of the confessional, I again heard words such as these: **My image already is in your soul. I desire that there be a Feast of Mercy. I want this image, which you will paint with a brush, to be solemnly blessed on the first Sunday after Easter; that Sunday is to be the Feast of Mercy.**
>
> *Diary*, 49

Christ even went so far as to reprimand her for delaying in fulfilling His command:

> **Know that if you neglect the matter of the painting of the image and the whole work of mercy, you will have to answer for a multitude of souls on the day of judgment.**
>
> *Diary*, 154

Poor Faustina. She tried, but she just couldn't do it. You need to understand that this was a simple

Polish peasant girl with only about three semesters of grammar school education — and art wasn't one of the courses offered. But Christ had appeared to her and told her to paint an image of Him.

As Fr. Seraphim Michalenko, MIC, explains:

> Faustina felt such an obligation to do something about the painting that she went to her superior and told her about it. Her superior said, "Here are canvas and paints. Go ahead and do it."
>
> Faustina said, "I don't know how to paint!"
>
> The sisters remember her putting paper on a wall, taking a piece of charcoal, and trying to draw the figure of Christ, but it just was not working.
>
> She learned that one of the nuns was a painter and used to make beautiful cards with little flowers, etc. So Faustina asked her to paint an image of Christ. The nun said, "I can only paint flowers; I'm not a portrait painter."
>
> Already the word was going out that she was having some kind of vision. She didn't do it to make herself known, but because she felt so compelled to fulfill the Lord's

wishes, and she couldn't do it.

She had no success until she got to Vilnius and finally met the spiritual director that the Lord intended for her, and he, after a long, long time, decided to help her and find an artist.

(So if you, like me, have ever wondered why the Lord couldn't make things a little easier for you, relax; you're in good company.)

What becomes clear from all this is that, to God, the Divine Mercy Image is a big deal. He wanted it painted, and He wanted it displayed so that people would see it. He wanted to make His mercy visible.

Since the first painting of the Divine Mercy Image (the Vilnius image), completed under Faustina's direction in 1934, many artists have attempted to capture the vision of Jesus seen by St. Faustina. Arguably, the Divine Mercy Image has now become the best-known and most widely-revered picture of Christ in the history of the Church.

So, what's the big deal? What's so special about this picture? Let's take a look.

Icon or Idol?

Over the years, questions (and even disputes) have arisen about why there are so many versions of the Image and which one is the "right one."

The truth is that there is no "right one," but there is a right way and a wrong way to *view* it. The most important thing to remember is that the Divine Mercy Image must be viewed as an *icon*, not an *idol*.

What's the difference? As I mentioned in the Foreword, an icon draws us *to* God. A true icon, according to the technical meaning of the term, is a very specific type of painting that symbolically represents Christ, the Mother of God, angels, saints, or events of sacred history.

The painter, or iconographer, is specially trained in the traditional rules, techniques, and style of iconography, and is often appointed by a bishop. In preparing to create an icon, he attempts to open himself to the inspiration of the Holy Spirit as he prays, fasts, chooses the best materials, and anoints and blesses his paints. He is conscious that he is not simply painting; he is "writing" a holy image.

In a less formal sense, the word icon can be used to describe any sacred image that symbolically represents a divine figure or subject in such a way that it aids the viewer in contemplating the divine reality that is being symbolized.

An idol, on the other hand, draws us *away from* God. We usually think of an idol as an image or statue that we worship as if it possesses some sort of divine power. The idol itself becomes the object of our attention and of our worship.

But anything can become an idol. Any object, person, idea, or cause that draws our attention and our worship to itself and away from God is an idol.

The difference, then, between an icon and an idol is that an icon does not become the object of our worship. Rather, it leads us beyond itself into a state of contemplation. Like a window, it allows us to look through it, so that with the eyes of our soul we see God. As St. Basil the Great wrote, "The honor rendered to the image passes to the prototype, because the person who venerates the icon venerates the person represented in it."

How does this relate to the Divine Mercy Image?

Though most versions of the Divine Mercy Image are not true icons, each is a sacred image intended to lead us, through contemplation, into the presence of Jesus Christ, who *is* Divine Mercy.

So our focus, as we take a "closer look" at the Divine Mercy Image, is not on the artwork itself, but on the truths, the theology, the "story" that it reveals.

Who's in the Picture?

Sometimes, when I'm giving a talk about the Image, I begin by asking a question that seems rather obvious. Gesturing to whatever version of the painting is displayed in the church or hall, I ask, "Who's this a picture of?"

I always get the same answers: "Jesus" ... "The Son of God" ... "Christ" ... "The Lord."

I smile, and respond:

> Yeeesss, ... of course. Now look again. Who *else* is it?

I get a lot of blank stares and wrinkled foreheads (and, perhaps, your brow is a bit furrowed, too).

Yes, it's the image of Christ, the Merciful Savior. But St. Paul tells us that Christ is "the *image* of the invisible God" (Col 1:15; emphasis added).

Who's this "invisible God"? The Father.

In his encyclical letter, *Rich in Mercy*, Pope John Paul II writes that Christ has made the Father known to us "in the most profound mystery of His being." The Father's "invisible nature," he explains, "becomes visible in Christ and through Christ, ... especially visible in His mercy" (#2).

The Pope goes on to stress that Christ doesn't simply talk about or explain mercy, but "makes it incarnate":

> He, Himself, ... *is* mercy. To the person who sees it in Him — and finds it in Him — God becomes "visible" in a particular way *as the Father who is rich in mercy.*
>
> *Rich in Mercy,* #2

As it is stated simply in the concluding section of the encyclical, God the Father "allows us to 'see' Him in Christ" (#15).

Remember what we saw in Secret 1, when Philip asks Jesus to show them the Father, and Jesus replies,

"He who has seen me has seen the Father" (Jn 14:9)? Sometimes I hear a paraphrase of this exchange with Philip echoing in my mind, intermingled with some of Christ's other teachings about His relationship with the Father. It's as if I'm Philip, and Christ is talking to me, in person, gently reprimanding me:

> Philip, don't you know? You've been with Me so long, and you still don't get it? How can you say, "Show us the Father"? When you see Me, you *see* the Father!
>
> The Father and I are *one*, Philip! *I'm* in *Him* and *He's* in *Me*. I don't do my own will. I do the will of the one who sent Me. And the one who sent Me has not left Me alone, because I *always* do what is pleasing to *Him*.
>
> I'm *always* showing you the Father, Philip. He *lives* in Me; and in everything I say and do, you see *Him* doing His work.
>
> See Jn 14:8-10; 6:38; 8:29

To Jesus, *everything* is about the Father. The driving force of His *whole life* is the Father. He lives to please the Father, to rejoice in the Father, to fulfill the Father's plan. He came to show us the Father, to reveal to us that His Father is rich in mercy. As Pope John Paul II expresses it, "Making the Father present as love and mercy is ... the fundamental touchstone of His mission as the Messiah" (*Rich in Mercy*, #3).

So, yes, the Divine Mercy Image is a picture of Jesus. But it's Jesus showing us the Father. What's He showing us? Let's take a look. Just call to mind the Image, or, even better, have it in front of you, and let's see what the different features of this "icon" show us.

The Hands Tell the Story

Fr. George Kosicki loved to evangelize with the Image, and he'd always begin the same way. "Look at the hands. The hands tell the story."

So, first, let's look at the right hand:

> See how it's forming a fist? ... No? Okay, look again. Now it's kind of cupped and held off to the side, as if He's about to slap you. ... No? Okay, look one more time. See how the fingers are holding a pencil, as if He's writing down your transgressions?

Pretty silly. But sometimes it's helpful to look at what's *not* there, and then you get a better understanding of why something else *is* there.

What *is* that right hand doing? It's blessing. As St. Faustina records in her account, Christ is raising up His hand in a "gesture of blessing" (*Diary*, 47). And there are reasons for that — a lot of reasons.

One of the things I love about art is that it captures and "freezes" a moment in time. In the Divine Mercy Image, that right hand is frozen. You can look at it all you want, but you can't change it. You can't turn it into a fist; you can't turn it into a hand that's about to slap you; you can't turn it into a hand holding a pencil, as if God is "checking you twice" and writing down whether you've been "naughty or nice." It is a hand that is *always* blessing and *only* blessing.

But what does the word *blessing* mean? Here again is a Christian term that we use all the time but perhaps don't fully understand. Does it just mean having *nice thoughts* toward someone? Sending out *good vibes*? What *is* blessing?

Let's check the *Catechism*:

> Blessing is a divine and life-giving action ... .
>
> #1078

Divine and *life-giving*. So blessing is something that a divine being does, and what He's doing is giving *life*. Wow! Think about that the next time someone sneezes and you say, "God bless you!" You're participating in a "divine and life-giving action." (More about that later.)

OK. A little pop quiz to see if you've been paying attention. In the Divine Mercy Image, who's doing the blessing?

Jesus, of course. As Pope Benedict XVI said, "Christ is, in person, the divine Blessing for the world." But, as we noted earlier, Christ came to fulfill the Father's will; in everything Christ does, we see the Father at work in Him. So who's the ultimate source of this divine blessing?

The Father. With His hand raised in blessing, Jesus shows us what the *Father* is doing — *all the time*.

Let's look at the rest of that *Catechism* quote:

> Blessing is a divine and life-giving

action, *the source of which is the Father*. ... The *Father* is acknowledged and adored as the source and the end of *all the blessings* of creation and salvation. In his Word who became incarnate, died, and rose for us, he *fills us with his blessings*. Through his Word, he pours into our hearts the Gift that contains all gifts, the Holy Spirit.

#1078, 1082; emphasis added

So *all blessing comes from the Father* who, through Jesus, pours the Holy Spirit into our hearts. Who's the Holy Spirit?

"The Lord, the giver of life" ... the one in whom the inscrutable Triune God *communicates himself to human beings*, constituting in them the source of eternal life.

The Lord and Giver of Life, # 1

Alright, back to that right hand. We now know that it's the Father's hand raised over us in blessing. And the Image shows us this action "frozen" in time, remember? The Father's hand is *always* blessing and *only* blessing:

> From the beginning until the end of time the whole of God's work is a *blessing*, … one vast divine blessing.
>
> *Catechism*, #1079

Isn't that awesome? Imagine meeting God the Father in an elevator. You want to make some conversation, so you say, "Hi! What do you do for work?" And he says, "I bless."

That's God's *whole work!* It's what He's doing *all the time!* Everything that comes from the hand of God is a blessing (yes, even if it doesn't always feel like it). All God wants to do is bless His children, pouring His own life into them, His own holiness into them, so they can be with Him forever.

I remember talking about this at a week-long Divine Mercy conference in Ireland several years ago, a workshop for priests and leaders in Divine Mercy. About a year later, I received a letter from one of the participants. She told me that she couldn't get the image of that hand out of her mind. Everywhere she went, no matter what she did, no matter what happened in her life, she kept seeing the Father's hand raised over her in blessing. And she wanted me to know how that image had changed her life, filling her with new peace and trust and a new sense of belonging to God. May that image stay with you as well!

The Hand of the Priest

When we consider that hand raised in blessing together with one of the other features of the painting, we learn another important truth. It's not just Christ who passes on the Father's blessing.

In the Divine Mercy Image, Jesus is dressed in a white garment. Some artists have chosen to tinge it with blue or various other colors, but Faustina made it very clear to the original artist that it's supposed to be white. What's that all about?

It's the white garment of the priesthood. This is Jesus, the one great High Priest. The *only* priest. All others share in the *one priesthood of Christ*. So it's very fitting that Christ's hand is raised in blessing, because in both Jewish and Christian tradition, the first function of the priest is to bless.

I remember hearing a teaching once that, in the

Jewish priesthood, if a priest refused to bless someone, he was cast out; his priesthood was gone, because he was refusing to fulfill his essential duty. He *had* to bless.

And in our Catholic tradition, the priest acts *in persona Christi,* in the person of Christ. The Father, who is perpetually blessing us in Christ, continues to extend that blessing through the priest. How appropriate, then, that we call each priest "Father"!

Have you ever been to a priestly ordination? It's like a wedding in a lot of ways. Traditionally, after a wedding ceremony, everyone lines up to greet the bride and groom. After an ordination, everyone lines up in a similar way.

What are they lining up for? The priest's *first blessing* — because that's who he now is, forever. "You are a *priest* forever." You are a *blesser* forever. The whole task of a priest is to bless; all his ministry is actually a form of blessing. That's what he's called to do: to pass on the Father's blessing.

The priest, as an ordained minister, shares fully in the priesthood of Christ, and thus in His ministry of blessing. But you and I are called to bless, too. In a very different but nonetheless real way, we are all called to share in the priesthood of Christ, all called to reflect and pass on the Father's love. As St. Peter tells us, "You are a chosen people, a royal priesthood" (1 Pet 2:9, NIV). And the *Catechism* teaches:

> The faithful, who by Baptism are incorporated into Christ and integrated into the People of God, are made sharers in their particular way in the priestly, prophetic, and kingly office of Christ, and have their own part to play in the mission of the whole Christian people. ... Lay people *share in Christ's priesthood.*
>
> #897, 941; emphasis added

I mentioned earlier that, when you say, "God bless you," you participate in a divine action. When a father and mother bless their children, for example, they are passing on the life-giving blessing of God the Father.

I began blessing my kids while they were still in the womb. I'd simply place my hand over my wife's belly and ask God to let His blessings fall upon the child within. And there were times, as the kids were growing older, when I was especially conscious of the Father blessing them through me.

I'd sneak up to their beds at night and raise my hands over them in blessing — especially when I felt I had failed in some way as a father. And I'd pray, "Father, fill up in them what was lacking from me."

The Invitation

Okay, so that's the right hand of blessing. What's the left hand tell us? Faustina writes that the left hand was "touching the garment at the breast," and that the garment was "slightly drawn aside" (*Diary*, 47). Her spiritual director, Blessed Michael Sopocko, who assisted her in giving directions to the artist she commissioned to paint the Image, added a few specific details, based on what she had told him.

He explained that the thumb and index finger of Christ's left hand are "*drawing open* the garment in the area of the heart," which is not visible.

What's this all about? It's a gesture of *invitation*. This is Christ, inviting us to come into His Heart, to rest in His Heart. And, like that "frozen" hand of blessing, this gesture, too, is permanent and unchangeable.

As Mother Teresa reminds us, Christ says, "'Come to Me.' Nowhere does the Gospel say, 'Go away,' but always 'Come to me.'" And Scripture records Christ's tender invitation:

> Come to me, all you who are weary and burdened, and I will give you rest.
>
> Mt 11:28, NIV

This invitation of the left hand may not seem significant, especially in light of all that we've just seen about what the right hand tells us. But this simple gesture of opening and inviting expresses a profound and virtually incomprehensible reality: the mystery of God's unlimited and unfathomable mercy.

God is always ready to open the garment of His Heart to let you and me in. We are each invited, called, welcomed — at each moment, no matter what we've done — to draw near to the Heart of God.

And the hands are not working independently. The movements of Christ's hands are "frozen" together, captured in simultaneous action. Together these hands do, indeed, tell us the essential "story" of mercy, the story we most need to hear and understand, the story of how loved we are by God.

The right hand tells us that all the Father wants to do is bless His children; the left shows us the actual source of that blessing and invites us to come and receive it as it pours out upon us through the open Heart of Christ.

Which leads us to the next feature of the Image:

Streams of Mercy

> From beneath the garment, slightly drawn aside at the breast, there were emanating two large rays, one red, the other pale.
>
> *Diary*, 47

Here, we have the most striking feature of the Divine Mercy Image and the feature that most sets it apart from all the other images of Christ: the rays of mercy streaming from Christ's Heart.

What are these rays all about? What do *they* tell us? I guess the best place to start is the explanation given by Christ Himself.

St. Faustina records that, at one point, her confessor instructed her to ask Jesus the meaning of the two rays. When she asked Him, the Lord responded:

> **The two rays denote Blood and Water. The pale ray stands for the Water which makes souls righteous. The red ray stands for the Blood which is the life of souls. ...**
>
> **These two rays issued forth from the very depths of My tender mercy when My agonized Heart was opened by a lance.**
>
> *Diary,* 299

The most obvious scriptural passage that this brings to mind is, of course, the powerful scene from John's Gospel when blood and water gushed forth from the pierced Heart of Jesus on the Cross:

> One of the soldiers pierced His side with a lance, and immediately there came out blood and water.
>
> Jn 19:34, NJB

But there are other passages that come to mind as well. Here we see the fulfillment of Christ's promise of "Living Water" and our rebirth in the Holy Spirit:

Whoever drinks of the water that I shall give him will never thirst; the water that I shall give him will become in him a spring of water welling up to eternal life.

Jn 4:14

Truly, truly, I say to you, unless one is born of water and the Spirit, he cannot enter the kingdom of God.

Jn 3:5

The Pale Rays

So many levels of meaning, so much symbolism here! The pale rays are usually interpreted as representing the gift of the Holy Spirit and the Sacrament of Baptism (the water that "makes souls righteous"). But they can also be seen as a representation of another sacrament: the Sacrament of Reconciliation, because Confession is an extension of Baptism. As Pope Francis explains:

Baptism is the "door" of faith and Christian life. ... Regenerated by water and the Holy Spirit, we are illuminated by grace which dispels the darkness of sin. ... The door to a new life is opened and the mercy of God enters our lives.

The Sacrament of Penance or Confession is, in fact, like a "second baptism" that refers back always to the first to strengthen and renew it. ...

I cannot be baptized many times, but I can go to Confession and by doing so renew the grace of Baptism. ...

Audience, November 13, 2013

The Red Rays

The red rays clearly represent the Eucharist (the blood that's the "life of souls"). In the Old Testament, Moses, just before going up the mountain to receive the Ten Commandments, sprinkled the people with the blood of the sacrifice, proclaiming it as "the blood of the covenant" (Ex 24:8).

And now here, in the pouring out of these red rays, we see a clear, visual reminder of Christ, the new Moses (and the new sacrificial lamb), fulfilling on the Cross His gift of the Eucharist at the Last Supper, when He proclaimed "the *new covenant*" in

His blood (see Lk 22:20). We hear this proclamation again at Mass, as Christ speaks to us through the priest:

> This is the chalice of my Blood, the Blood of the new and eternal covenant, which will be poured out for you and for many for the forgiveness of sins.
>
> *Roman Missal*, 90

But, like the pale rays, the red rays can be seen as representing another sacrament as well. And again, it's Confession, because, as we've just seen, Christ's blood is being poured out *for the forgiveness of sins* — forgiveness that was won for us by the shedding of His blood on the Cross and that becomes available to us in the confessional.

Christ reveals to St. Faustina,

> **When you go to Confession, to this fountain of My mercy, the Blood and Water which came forth from My Heart always flows down upon your soul and ennobles it.**
>
> *Diary*, 1602

Self-Emptying Love

The rays also speak to us of God's *self-emptying love*. Nowhere is this love more completely expressed and manifested than at the piercing of Christ's Heart on the Cross.

Jesus has been bleeding for hours — from the thorns cutting into His head, from the open wounds where the scourges tore His flesh, from the nail holes in His hands and feet.

Now, with the piercing of His Heart, He is not just bleeding; He is bled out. The blood and water gushing from that tender Heart represents the complete outpouring of Christ's life blood. He has held nothing back; He has given all.

This is mercy! This is the self-emptying of God, the complete self-giving of the Father to His children. As Pope Benedict XVI expresses it, this is "the turning of God against himself" for love of us.

> For God so loved the world that he gave his only-begotten Son, that whoever

believes in him should not perish but have eternal life.

Jn 3:16

That's what you're worth to God. That's how much He loves you. That's the story of mercy that these rays tell us.

Heart of Mercy

As we saw earlier, Christ told St. Faustina, **"These two rays issued forth from the very depths of My tender mercy when My agonized Heart was opened by a lance on the Cross"** (*Diary*, 299).

But wait. The heart isn't visible in this image, remember? Why isn't it? In the Sacred Heart Image, based on Christ's appearances to St. Margaret Mary, the heart is visible in great detail: a wounded heart on a throne of flames below a cross, surrounded by a crown of thorns.

In Christ's words to Faustina, He refers to His pierced Heart. Why isn't it visible in His appearance to her? Why this significant difference between the central images of the Sacred Heart devotion and the Divine Mercy devotion?

I wouldn't presume to give a definitive answer, but to me it's a matter of focus and of Christ's gradual but constant "unpacking" of the message of merciful love that He came to reveal. The Divine Mercy devotion can be seen as a continuation and extension of the Sacred Heart devotion.

This first became clear to me at a "Fortnight of Mercy" that I was helping to present at the National Shrine of The Divine Mercy in the early nineties.

One of the speakers began by calling our attention to the large Divine Mercy Image that was displayed at the front of the room.

"I'm sure you are all familiar with this Divine Mercy Image," he began, "and you know that these red and pale rays represent the endless fountain of mercy that gushed forth from the Heart of Jesus.

"You probably can't see from where you are," he said, "but if you were to look closely at the bottom right corner of this image, you would notice a tiny dial. Right now, it's turned all the way to the right."

We all smiled, knowing that there was no dial; but

he had our attention. Where was he going with this?

"If you were to turn the dial all the way to the left," he continued, "the image would change dramatically. The rays would withdraw back into Christ's chest; the garment would open fully; and Christ's wounded Heart would become clearly visible, with its flames of love and crown of thorns. The Divine Mercy Image would become the Sacred Heart Image.

"The Sacred Heart Image," he explained, "shows us the *source* of mercy; the Divine Mercy Image shows us the *distribution* of mercy." Both show us the merciful love of God, but each has it's own primary focus.

When I think of the Sacred Heart devotion, the word that comes to me is *lamentation*. In Christ's revelations to St. Margaret Mary in 1675, we hear what, to me, are the "Lamentations of the Lover."

Behold this Heart which has so loved men that it spared nothing, even going so far as to exhaust and consume Itself to prove to them Its love. In return, I receive from the greater part of men nothing but ingratitude, by the contempt, irreverence, sacrileges, and coldness with which they treat Me … .

This is Christ crying out for us to understand how much He loves us, how personally He feels all our sufferings, and how deeply grieved He is by our sins, our ingratitude, and our rejection of His love, which only seeks our good.

He promised St. Margaret Mary that He would pour out all the treasures of His Heart upon those who would seek to return His love, honoring and consoling His wounded Heart.

It is the fulfillment of this promise that we see in the Divine Mercy Image. As Jesus explained to Sr. Josepha Menendez of the Society of the Sacred Heart,

> How often in the course of the ages have I, in one way or another, made known My love for men: I have shown them how ardently I desire their salvation. I have revealed My Heart to them. …
>
> *Now I want something more*, for if I long for love in response to My own, this is not the only return I desire from souls: I want

them all to have *confidence in My mercy*, to expect all from My clemency, and never to doubt My readiness to forgive.

To me everything hinges on the word *response*. Jesus revealed Himself in each of these ways (first in the Sacred Heart Image and then in the Divine Mercy Image) for a *reason*. What does He want from us? What *response* does each image call forth from us?

As we view the Sacred Heart of Jesus, so terribly wounded for us, we are called to respond by *returning His love, seeking to console His Heart and make reparation* for the ways in which it has been so grievously offended.

As we view the Image of Divine Mercy, we are called to respond by *embracing the blessing*, realizing that the best way to make reparation and console the Heart of Jesus is to *receive* His mercy with gratitude and expectant faith, *placing all our trust in Him.*

(For a much deeper and more complete treatment of this, see Fr. Michael Gaitley's *Consoling the Heart of Jesus* and Dr. Robert Stackpole's *Divine Mercy: A Guide from Genesis to Benedict XVI.*)

You Rays Me Up

I want to go back for a moment to that imaginary dial that controls the outflow or inflow of the rays in the Divine Mercy Image.

Several years ago, I received a letter from a man who had happened upon a magazine that featured the Divine Mercy Image on the cover, keyed to an article I had written. He said that he had never really accepted God and had never even thought about having a personal relationship with Him. But for some reason, the rays on the image had caught his attention.

He said that he kept seeing the rays in reverse, not as something coming out, but as a pathway leading up and in. Then, suddenly, he felt himself being pulled through the rays into the picture. It totally converted him.

His letter reminded me of something I had often experienced, not from looking at the Image, but from meditating on the Passion of Christ — especially the wound in His side. I would imagine being at the foot of the Cross with Mary and John and experiencing the blood and water coming down upon me and pulling me right up into that wound.

It was a powerful image for me and brought me great consolation, especially when I was having a difficult time. I just imagined myself being absorbed right into that wound in Christ's side and resting in His Heart: Safe. Loved. Protected.

That mental image later evolved into what I call the "Tabernacle Prayer," because in the tabernacle we find the Merciful Heart of Jesus, waiting for us, waiting to love and heal and fill us with peace.

As I wrote in *21 Ways to Worship,*

> Now, anytime I feel that the world is getting to me too much, anytime I start to feel too overwhelmed, too burdened, too anxious, too depressed, too exhausted, too caught up in myself, I just mentally approach the tabernacle and ask Jesus to lock me in there with Him. There, I experience the peace that passes understanding, the peace that only God can give. There I remember, "Oh, yeah, You're God. You're all I need. You can handle everything."

And I'm not alone. Faustina writes:

> From the time I left the novitiate, I have enclosed myself in the tabernacle together with Jesus, my Master. He himself drew me into the fire of living love on which everything converges.
>
> *Diary*, 704

The Signature: Covenant of Mercy

And that brings us to the words that the Lord insisted must be inscribed at the bottom of the Divine Mercy Image: "Jesus, I trust in You!"

Trust in God is the essence of the message of mercy. Over and over again, Christ insisted on the necessity of trust and urged St. Faustina to encourage all souls to trust in His mercy (see *Diary*, 1182, 1578).

One of the root meanings of the word *trust* is agreement, or pact. And, throughout both the Old and New Testaments, God has made it clear that this is what He wants from us — not an agreement in the sense of a legal contract, but in the sense of establishing a family bond through a covenant relationship based on love and trust: "You will be my people, and I will be your God" (Ez 36:28, NIV).

As Dr. Scott Hahn explains,

> Contractual relations usually exchange property, exchange goods and services, whereas covenants exchange persons. So when people enter into a covenant, they say, "I am yours and you are mine."

Trust means we accept this covenant relationship, that we agree to let God be our Father. (It's the antidote to the first sin of Adam!) It means that we agree that He can write the script of our lives, instead of insisting on our own script. It means that we agree with the great pledge we make in the Lord's Prayer: that *His* will — not ours — may be done "on earth as it is in heaven."

This covenant with God is made very clear in the *Diary*. In the famous first revelation on February 22, 1931, when Jesus appears to Sr. Faustina with the rays of mercy streaming from His Heart, He tells her to paint a picture of this vision, "with the signature, 'Jesus, I trust in You'" (*Diary*, 47).

The word *signature* is important here. What Jesus is presenting to us is a covenant of mercy to be *signed* with our trust. The image is a visual reminder that Jesus has already fulfilled His part in this covenant. As the one, eternal High Priest, He has already signed it with His blood, offering the perfect sacrifice and redeeming us from our sins "once for all" (Heb 9:26). Forgiveness and reconciliation with the Father have already been won for all our sins — past, present, and future.

How do we fulfill our part of the covenant? By opening our hearts in trust to Jesus. The more complete our trust, the more we open ourselves to receive all the blessings He wants to pour out upon us.

Faustina gives us a perfect example of this. Four years after her first revelation, on February 4, 1935, she reached a new level in her trust relationship with Christ and symbolically "signed" her personal covenant of mercy with God in a very concrete way.

She was making a retreat in Vilnius and, in the evening, our Lord told her, **"You will cancel out your will absolutely in this retreat. ... My complete will shall be accomplished in you"** (*Diary*, 372).

He then gave her detailed instructions:

> Write these words on a clean sheet of paper: "From today on, my own will does not exist," and then cross out the page. And on the other side write these words: "From today on, I do the will of God everywhere, always, and in everything."
>
> *Diary,* 372

On the next two pages of the *Diary,* Sr. Faustina fulfilled the Lord's request and recorded for us the immediate response she received from God:

> The moment I knelt down to cross out my own will, as the Lord had bid me to do, I heard this voice in my soul: "From today on, do not fear God's judgment, for you will not be judged."
>
> *Diary,* 374

Like Sr. Faustina, we, too, are called to grow in trust by placing ourselves completely in God's hands, seeking His will, not our own.

Every time we say the prayer, "Jesus, I trust in You," we should be re-signing our covenant with

God, renewing our commitment to really trust in His moment-to-moment will in our lives, realizing that His will is Love and Mercy Itself.

The Conversion Prayer

At this point, I need to share something. I was in my early teens when I was introduced to the Divine Mercy devotion. I learned about the "conversion prayer," the prayer for sinners that consoled Jesus most, and that He promised to answer (see *Diary*, 1397):

> **When you say this prayer, with a contrite heart and with faith on behalf of some sinner, I will give him the grace of conversion. This is the prayer: "O Blood and Water, which gushed forth from the Heart of Jesus as a fount of Mercy for us, I trust in You."**
>
> *Diary*, 186-187

So I began praying this prayer, but it felt a little weird. "I'm praying to blood and water? I'm trusting in blood and water? I don't want to pray to blood and water; I want to pray to Jesus. I want to trust in Him."

Then I came across this passage from the *Diary*:

> I received an inner understanding about the inscription. Jesus reminded me … that these three words must be clearly in evidence: "Jesus, I trust in You." ["Jezu, Ufam Tobie."] I understood that Jesus wanted the whole formula to be there, but He gave no direct orders to this effect.
>
> *Diary*, 327

The whole formula. The full "O Blood and Water" prayer is what Jesus really wanted at the bottom of the Image. But as long as the words, "Jesus, I trust in You" were there, it was enough.

I suddenly realized that it's the same thing. The Blood and Water that gushed forth from the Heart of Jesus *is* Jesus. He's pouring *Himself* into us, His very life, His whole being! It's *Jesus* whom I'm trusting.

The Dialogue of Abandonment

Pope John Paul II, whose first proclamation to the world as pope was "Be not afraid," refers to this covenant as a "dialogue of abandonment" that enables us to let go of all our fears, concerns, doubts, anxieties, and just put everything in God's hands.

We're each called to a private dialogue with God. What's God's part in the dialogue? To tell us not to be afraid. What's our response? "Jesus, I trust in You!"

> Anyone can come here, look at this image of the merciful Jesus, … and hear in the depths of his own soul what Blessed Faustina heard: "Fear nothing. I am with you always" (*Diary*, 586).
>
> And if this person responds with a sincere heart: "Jesus, I trust in You," he will find comfort in all his anxieties and fears. In this "dialogue of abandonment," there is established between man and Christ a special bond that sets love free. And "there is no fear in love, but perfect love casts out fear" (1 Jn 4:18).
>
> Pope John Paul II, Shrine of The Divine Mercy
> Poland, June 7, 1997

Mercy in Motion

There's another feature of the Image that is often

overlooked. If you look just above that signature at the bottom, you'll see that even Christ's feet and stance speak to us of His mercy.

According to Fr. Sopocko, St. Faustina instructed that Christ's left foot should be slightly forward of the right to show that He is in a walking position, and that His "entire frontal position" should exhibit and impart peace. Fr. Sopocko continues:

> The image should portray Christ at the moment of the institution of the Sacrament of Penance with the words, "Peace to you!" ... the guiding thought that runs through every page of the *Diary* — **"Mankind will not find peace until it turns with trust to My Mercy"** (*Diary*, 300).

God is never just "sitting around" waiting for us to seek Him. He is mercy in motion, always seeking us, always moving toward us, always wanting to be close to us and fill us with the peace "that surpasses all understanding" (Phil 4:7 NABRE).

As Pope John Paul II explains:

> In Jesus Christ, God not only speaks to

man but also *seeks him out*. ... God goes in search of man, created in his own image and likeness, ... because he loves him eternally in the Word, and wishes to raise him in Christ to the dignity of an adoptive son. ... God seeks man out, moved by his fatherly heart.

As the Third Millennium Draws Near, #7; emphasis original

The Gaze of Mercy

One of the most difficult tasks for the original artist (and, it seems, for later artists as well) was to capture the gentle, loving expression that Faustina saw on Christ's face when He appeared to her. As Fr. Sopocko explains, she insisted that the expression on Christ's face be "loving and merciful," that His eyes not "bore into" the viewer, but be "directed somewhat downwards," and that His gaze should be merciful "as from the Cross."

Christ, Himself had told her,

My gaze from this image is like My gaze from the Cross.

Diary, 326

So, the artist had to continually redo the face, but he never succeeded in pleasing her. Finally she came in, stating that the image was ugly, but that the Lord had told her to leave it as it was, saying, "It's not good, but it will do."

She later wrote that, at one point, she went into the chapel and cried, asking the Lord, "Who will paint You as beautiful as you are?" He replied, **"Not in the beauty of the color, nor of the brush lies the greatness of this image, but in My grace"** (*Diary*, 313).

I think it's important to ask for that grace. No matter which version of the Image we look at, no matter how well or how poorly the artist succeeded in capturing the merciful gaze of Christ, we need to ask for the grace to look beyond the painted image and see the actual face of Christ, see His loving gaze.

It was this gaze that penetrated the heart of Zaccheus, the publican, and changed his life forever (see Lk 19:5-6). That same gaze fell upon Peter after His denial of Jesus and caused him to weep tears of repentance (see Lk 22:61-62). And it was the experience of this gaze of mercy that called Pope Francis to enter religious life.

Indeed, when the Pope was asked in an interview in 2013, "Who is Jorge Mario Bergolio?" he said, "I am a sinner whom the Lord has *looked upon*."

Mother Teresa felt that experiencing this gaze was so important that she wrote about it in a letter to the Missionaries of Charity just before she died:

> Jesus wants me to tell you … how much love He has for each one of you — beyond all you can imagine. I worry some of you still have not really met Jesus — one to one — you and Jesus alone. We may spend time in chapel — but *have you seen with the eyes of your soul how He looks at you with love?* Do you really know the living Jesus? …
>
> He loves you, but even more — He longs for you. He misses you when you don't come close. He thirsts for you. He loves you always, even when you don't feel worthy. When not accepted by others, even by yourself sometimes — He is the one who always accepts you.

In declaring the Extraordinary Jubilee of Mercy, Pope Francis writes that Jesus "is the *face* of the

Father's mercy. ... For all eternity man will always be under the merciful gaze of the Father"(*Face of Mercy*, #1, 7). And, as if he were looking at the Divine Mercy Image, he continues:

> With our eyes fixed on Jesus and his *merciful gaze*, we experience the love of the Most Holy Trinity. The mission Jesus received from the Father was that of *revealing the mystery of divine love in its fullness*. ...
>
> This love has now been made *visible and tangible* in Jesus' entire life. His person is nothing but love. ... Everything in him speaks of mercy. Nothing in him is devoid of compassion.
>
> *Face of Mercy*, #8

The Divine Mercy Image is not just a picture of Jesus for *us to look at*. It's, in a very real sense, an icon that helps us enter into the reality of *the way God looks at us*, that helps us see with our inner eyes *the way God loves*, and thus come to know our Father God as He is, "merciful and gracious, slow to anger and abounding in steadfast love" (Ps 103:8, NRSV).

$\mathscr{S}$ECRET 4

God Loves Backwards

**I am more generous toward sinners
than toward the just.**

Jesus to St. Faustina

In the last chapter, we saw that, among other things, the Divine Mercy Image can help us come to a deeper understanding of how God loves us and, thus, to place our trust in Him.

But the picture isn't meant to do that all by itself. It's to draw us deeper into God's revelations throughout the ages, to remind us of what He's been trying to tell us all along — through the Scriptures, the teachings of the Church, and the saints, especially, in our time, St. Faustina.

Lifting the Veil

Faustina had a sense that her mission was to lift the veils that prevent us from really seeing and understanding this essential message of Divine Mercy: *God loves you; trust Him.*

Faustina knew that these two things are related. We don't really understand how God loves; therefore, we don't completely trust in Him. So she took on a mission to lift the veils so that we could really see God as He is and thus stop wounding Him by our lack of trust:

> O God, how I desire that souls come to know You and to see that You have created them because of Your unfathomable love. O my Creator and Lord, I feel that I am going to remove the veil of heaven so that earth will not doubt Your goodness.
>
> *Diary*, 483

She was convinced that this would be her mission forever, both on earth and in Heaven:

> I feel certain that my mission will not come to an end upon my death, but will begin. O doubting souls, I will draw aside for you the veils of heaven to convince you of God's goodness, so that you will no longer continue to wound with your distrust the sweetest Heart of Jesus.
>
> *Diary*, 281

To me, the main "veil" that needs to be lifted is our tendency to assume that God loves the way we do.

The Book of Genesis (1:26-27) tells us that God created us in His image and likeness, and yet we keep trying to re-create Him in ours. We keep thinking that He must be like us, must think like us, must perceive things like us, must love (and hate) like us, must get angry and resentful like us.

But that results in a distorted view of who God is and who we are. He's not like *us*. We're supposed to be like *Him*. That's why He created us, remember? To be like Him so that we can be with Him forever. And so, He is always loving us, calling us, and trying to help us become who He created us to be.

We say we believe that God is loving and forgiving, but so often it's just a thought, just a pious concept that stays in our heads. We just don't *get it*, deep down, with a gut knowledge, a heart knowledge, a life-changing sureness that God really does love *me* that much and that He's going to stick with me through everything.

We don't understand, or we forget; and so we are never fully at peace, never fully at rest, but seem always a bit frayed around the edges: anxious, stressed, insecure, lonely, preoccupied with "important" things that we may not even remember later. As the poet Bryant wrote in "Thanatopsis," we each plod on from day to day, chasing our "favorite phantoms," searching for a happiness and peace that will always elude us until we learn to simply let our hearts rest in the tenderness of God.

What we need to realize is that, compared to the way we love, God loves backwards. Now, obviously, *we're* the ones who love backwards; but compared to us, compared to our whole concept of love, our whole way of loving, it seems as if God's got it all wrong.

"Behave Yourself!"

Let's take a look at how we love, and then compare that to the way God loves.

The first thing to realize is that love is not just an emotion, and it's not just something that "happens." For the most part, we don't *fall* in love (or fall out of love). We *learn* how to love. And, like anything that is learned, love can be learned well or badly, depending on how we're raised, what we experience, and, most especially, how we're treated by others.

Most of us learn to love, and to "earn" love from others, based on behavior. We learn that what we do (or don't do) affects the way other people respond:

> We learn early that parents, teachers, friends, even strangers react positively or negatively to us *based on how we act*. Even Santa Claus is checking up on us to see whether we've been "naughty or nice." If you're good, you get good things; if you're bad, all you get is coal in your stocking.

You say "yes" to mom and dad, and you get a smile. You say "no," and you get scowls and angry words (or you get called by your *full* name). Right from kindergarten on, the ones who do well get the gold stars, the pat on the back, the affirming looks, and the words of approval. We get rewarded or punished, loved or not loved, based on the "b" word: *behavior.*

I learned this *really* well. I learned that love is *conditional* (long before I even knew what that word meant). I learned to "behave myself," to say and do the things that would "earn" the love and approval of others. It became a kind of "hot and cold faucet" experience: people would be "hot" or "cold" to me depending on my behavior.

Naturally, since this was the way I learned to *receive* love, it also became the way I *gave* love. For much of my life, the people I tended to love most were those who loved me the most, those who treated me well or behaved according to my expectations.

God forgive me for the times I even treated my children this way, showing or withholding love based on how well they were obeying my "rules" or doing the things I thought were best for them.

Essentially what this distorted concept of love does is turn us into robots. We let *other people* choose how *we're* going to behave. You do something that bothers me; I react to what you did; then you react to my reaction; and we keep going back and forth, just bouncing off each other's behavior.

Neither of us actually sees the other as a person; neither of us chooses to care about the other. We simply see and react to the other's behavior.

Years ago, when I was trying to get this concept across to a psychology class I was teaching, I wrote a poem called "Buttons." The basic concept is that we all have buttons that control our actions, and the more you get to know someone, the more you learn which buttons to push to get the desired response.

Children are very good at this. They quickly learn which buttons to push, and they delight in it. It's a testing process they learn.

As we grow older we become more subtle about it, often manipulating each other without even con-sciously knowing or intending it. We need to "unlearn" that. We need to learn to focus on the person instead of the behavior.

Buttons

Shall I push the button that will make you Like me? Or the one to make you Hate?

Or perhaps, your Anger button, so I can watch you Frown and Sneer?

Or your Judge and Label button? Ah, That'll make you feel secure. Let's see ... Where shall I push you now?

Shall it be Sadness, Loneliness, or Pride? Confusion, Smiles, or Pain? Anxiety, or Mockery? Rejection, Doubt, or Fear?

There's such a huge selection! It's hard to make a choice!

Oh, wait ... what's this? So tiny ... I almost passed it by!

Oh, yes, here's the button I want, the button that will blow your buttons skyward, and leave you Buttonless — and Free!

© 1978 Vinny Flynn

God Is Buttonless

You see, that's the goal — to be buttonless. To be free to decide how you want to behave instead of letting others decide for you. To be free to love as God loves.

God doesn't have any buttons we can push to make Him behave in a particular way. God chooses how He's going to behave, and it's always the same choice. He doesn't love us only if we do something to "deserve" it. He always chooses to love. It's a choice He made before the world began, because love is His very nature:

> We look at our behavior and think we're unworthy of His love. Well, guess what? Of course you're unworthy of His love! He's God, and you're just a creature He created out of dust. What could you ever do to become worthy of His love?

> The good news is that you don't have to be worthy of His love. He loves you because of who He is and who He created you to be — not just a creature, but His own child.

You can't earn God's love, and you can't lose it; you already have it, forever.

Time for a Test

Let's look at a specific example. Here's a little quiz. You've got three friends:

Friend A: This is a forever friend, someone you can always count on, someone who would literally give you the shirt off his back, someone you know just loves you and will always be there for you.

Friend B: This is a sunshine friend. When everything's fine this is a good friend, but if things get rough, this is not someone you can count on to stick with you.

Friend C: This is a superficial friend, a kind of "hail fellow, well met" friend. Pleasant enough, but you know there's no real depth there, no real relationship.

Now, be honest. Which friend would tend to draw

your love most? Which one has the greatest right to your love? Most of us would choose Friend A, the forever friend. That's the one who would draw our love most, the one who *deserves* our love most.

But God doesn't love that way. Who would draw His love most? Friend C, the superficial friend, the one who doesn't deserve His love. Seems backwards, doesn't it?

Priority Access

In His revelations to St. Faustina, Christ makes this very clear:

> On the cross, the fountain of My mercy was opened wide by the lance for *all souls!* … Let no soul fear to draw near to Me, *even though its sins be as scarlet.*
>
> *Diary,* 1182, 699

> The greater the sinner, the greater the right he has to My mercy. … Let the greatest sinners place their trust in My mercy. They have the *right before others* to trust in the abyss of My mercy.
>
> *Diary,* 723, 1146

> I am more generous *toward sinners* than toward the just.
>
> *Diary*, 1275

> When a soul sees and realizes the gravity of its sins ... let it not despair, but with trust let it throw itself into the arms of My mercy. These souls have a *right of priority* to My compassionate Heart, they have *first access* to My mercy.
>
> *Diary*, 1541

Wow! That seems pretty extreme. The greatest sinners have the greatest right to His mercy? The right before others? He's more generous to them than to those who are living good lives? The worst sinners have priority rights? First access to His mercy? How do you feel about that? Does that seem right to you?

It brings to mind two Gospel stories that bothered me for a long time. They even made me angry.

One is the Prodigal Son story (Lk 15:11-32). I'm kind of with the elder son there a little bit. "Hey Dad, I've been keeping the rules, I stayed here and worked! I didn't go out and spend all the money, I didn't ask for my inheritance now. I'm the good one! I'm doing the good stuff, and you throw the party for that son of yours?!"

And then there's the story about the workers in the vineyard (Mt 20:1-15). "Hey, wait a minute! I've been slaving in the hot sun all day! This guy only worked for one hour, and he gets the same as me?!"

That's Just Not Fair

Ever get invaded by those subtle forms of envy and judgment that kinda creep in to us "good Christians" and cause us to think we're being cheated of something, or overlooked in some way? Cause us to feel angry or resentful because someone else is getting something we're not? Something we feel we deserve more than they do?

I don't know about you, but the phrase that used to come to my mind was, "That's just not fair!" Ever find yourself thinking or even saying that?

Well, it's a pun. It's an accurate statement if we add a comma and change the emphasis a bit. The phrase should be, "That's *just*, not *fair*."

This always reminds me of a teacher I had when I was in college. When he heard that I was getting married, he said,

> Look, when you start having kids, and the first one comes up and complains, "Daddy, that's not fair," you respond, "I promise you, I will never try to be fair, but I will always try to be just."

What does "fair" mean? When you say, "Daddy, that's not fair," what you're saying is, "You're treating him differently than you treat me." Fair means same. If I'm being fair, that means I'm treating everyone exactly the same way.

Well that's not just. I have seven kids. If I treat them all the same, I'm being unjust to at least six of them, because each one is a completely unique person! Different needs, different personalities, different wants, different ways of learning and understanding.

I love them all, but not just *all*. I love them *each*, and I love each *differently!* If I tried to treat them all the same, it would be a disaster. And it would be *unjust*.

In justice, as their father, I have a moral responsibility to be "faithful to my fatherhood" by respecting my children as individual persons, seeking to understand and respond to each in the best way possible in order to lead *them* to "act justly" and to seek harmony with each other. In justice — and in mercy, which "reveals the perfection of justice" — I have a responsibility to know and love each of my children in the same personal, self-giving, one-on-one way that God the Father loves me (see *Rich in Mercy*, #8).

Beyond Behavior

God knew and loved each of us ahead of time, remember? He chose each of us and knows each of us intimately. He seeks only our good, seeks only to bless us, restore us, and respond to our unique needs in order to draw us to Him. He looks beyond behavior, beyond situations, even beyond sin, and sees the person He created in love. As I wrote in *7 Secrets of Confession*,

> He sees everything — all our sins, all our weaknesses, even our most hidden thoughts — but He also sees the beautiful "not yet"

that even we, ourselves, may not see, the "not yet" of who we are but have not yet become. And with His searing, healing, all-embracing gaze of love, He calls us by name and invites Himself into our home.

I remember a bit of advice my brother Art gave to a family member who came to him for help in dealing with the way some of her co-workers were acting. It had become a real problem for her, and she was struggling to cope with it without anger and resentment. He told her,

You just need to love beyond behavior.

He himself lived that advice, witnessing to it on a daily basis. He would literally walk across the street to talk with the person whom most other people would cross the street to avoid. He saw all the negative, annoying stuff that everyone else saw, but he chose to love beyond it.

Pope Francis explains,

The call of Jesus pushes each of us never to stop at the surface of things, especially when we are dealing with a person. We are

called to look beyond, to focus on the heart
to see how much generosity everyone is
capable of.

No one can be excluded from the mercy
of God; everyone knows the way to access it
and the Church is *the house that welcomes all
and refuses no one.* Its doors remain wide
open, so that those who are touched by
grace can find the certainty of forgiveness.
The greater the sin, so much the greater
must be the love that the Church expresses.

Homily, March 13, 2015; emphasis original

Why do the greatest sinners have the greatest
right to God's mercy? Because they *need it most.* And
as Christ tells us in Scripture, He didn't come to save
the righteous, He came to save the sick. God knows
that sin is sickness, it's woundedness, it's misery, and
He knows all the things that can lead a person to sin.

As I mentioned earlier, you and I tend to focus on
behavior and to judge people — including ourselves
— based on whether we approve or don't approve of
that behavior. And that becomes our measuring
stick for giving or withholding love.

God isn't focused on our behavior; he's focused on our relationship with Him. He knows that our negative behavior, our sin, separates us from Him, weakens our relationship with Him. So He responds with what Pope Francis calls "the judgment of mercy ... the love that goes *beyond* justice" (March 13, 2015).

Christ doesn't mince words about this in the Gospel. He makes it unmistakably clear that He expects us to love the way He loves — and He gets very specific about it:

> Love your enemies, do good to those who hate you. ... If you love those who love you, what credit is that to you? For even sinners love those who love them. And if you do good to those who do good to you, what credit is that to you? For even sinners do the same. ...
>
> But love your enemies, and do good ... and you will be sons of the Most High; for he is kind to the ungrateful and the selfish.
>
> Be merciful, even as your Father is merciful. ... For the measure you give will be the measure you get back.
>
> Lk 6:27, 32-33, 35-36, 38

So that's the challenge for us. We need to understand the radical difference between the way God loves and the way we tend to love, and come around to his way. We need to learn to love "backwards."

$\mathscr{S}$ECRET 5
Prodigal Doesn't Mean Bad

**The very inner depths of My being
are filled to overflowing with mercy,
and it is being poured out upon all I have created.**

Jesus to St. Faustina

As a kid, I had no clue what *prodigal* meant. All I knew was that the younger son in the famous Parable of the Prodigal Son (see Lk 15:11-32) was a real mess.

So, I just unconsciously associated the word with what I had learned about the younger son, and to me

131

prodigal came to mean bad, rebellious, a real sinner.

Later on, I realized that the elder son was no bargain either. He was prodigal, too. And, much later, I finally realized that the story wasn't really about either of those kids. It was about their father (who clearly represents God the Father). *He* was the one who was the most prodigal. To me, this story is, more than anything else, the Parable of the Prodigal Father.

So what does it really mean to be *prodigal?* It means to "squander" (derived from the Latin *prodigere, prodigus,* meaning "squander" or "lavish"). Used in a negative sense, it means to squander or waste money or resources, to be rashly and recklessly extravagant.

The Prodigal Son

Obviously, that seems a pretty accurate description of the younger son, who asks for his inheritance ahead of time and then leaves his father's house and travels far from home. There he goes on a spending spree, having "a great time" as he wastes it all on loose living — only to suddenly discover that he's not really having such a great time after all:

> After a few days, the younger son collected all his belongings and set off to a distant country where he squandered his inheritance on a life of dissipation. When he had freely spent everything, a severe famine struck that country, and he found himself in dire need.
>
> *Lk 15:13-14, NABRE*

In leaving his father's house, he had lost all his money, all his possessions. But as Pope John Paul II writes in *Rich in Mercy,* he had also lost something of far greater value:

> The *inheritance* that the son had received from his father was a quantity of material goods, but more important than these goods was *his dignity as a son in his father's house.*
>
> *Rich in Mercy,* #5

What the son gradually comes to, the Pope continues, is "the awareness of squandered sonship, … the sense of lost dignity … that dignity that springs from the relationship of the son with the father" (#5).

Realizing that even the pigs he's caring for are eating better than he is, and that the servants in his father's house possess the basic material goods that he no longer has, the boy decides to return to his father and ask to be treated as a servant.

To have to earn your living by working as a servant in your own father's house would be a great humiliation, but, as Pope John Paul II points out, the son is willing to accept this because "he realizes that he no longer has any right except to be an employee in his father's house" (#5).

So he prepares a script for his return meeting with his father:

> I will arise and go to my father, and I will say to him, "Father, I have sinned against heaven and before you; I am no longer worthy to be called your son; treat me as one of your hired servants."
>
> Lk 15:18-19, RSV

The son has had a reality check. He is painfully aware of his sin, and knows that, in accordance with the norms of justice, he no longer deserves to be treated as a son; he has lost his right to sonship.

And that's the great lie! *We can't lose our sonship or daughtership.* Yes, unfortunately there are earthly parents who disown their children, who allow their children's behavior to cause them to destroy the bond of filial love. But *God never disowns His children.* He loves backwards, remember? He doesn't give us *less* love when we hurt Him; He gives us *more!*

The prodigal son is about to be surprised. He's learned about justice; he's about to learn about mercy.

The Prodigal Father

He sets out on the long road back to his father's house most likely rehearsing and re-rehearsing his script and wondering how his father is going to react. He gets home and bangs on the door until his father finally comes out. His father looks him over contemptuously from head to toe and says,

> "Ah, I knew you'd come sniveling back, you miserable whelp. Looks like you've had a rough time. Things didn't turn out too well for you, did they? Well, you got what you deserved, so you can just turn around

and go back where you came from. There's no longer any place for you here."

I know. That's not really what he said. But the reality is that there are times when parents *do* react this way, and, again, it sometimes helps to see what *wasn't* said in order to fully appreciate what *was* said.

The son didn't really knock on the door; he didn't have to:

> While he was still a long way off, his father saw him and was filled with compassion for him; he ran to his son, threw his arms around him and kissed him.
>
> LK 15:20, NIV

His father saw him while he was still "a long way off." Why? Because he was *looking*. Because he was *waiting*. But, when he saw his son, he didn't keep waiting. He *ran* to him, hugged him, kissed him. He didn't even let his son finish his rehearsed script, but cried out to his servants:

> Quick! Bring the best robe and put it on him. Put a ring on his finger and sandals on

his feet. Bring the fattened calf and kill it. Let's have a feast and celebrate. For this son of mine was dead and is alive again; he was lost and is found.

Lk 15:22-24, NIV

Pretty extreme reaction to the return of a wayward son, don't you think? This is not some returning hero. This is an ungrateful, rebellious son who turned away from his father and broke his heart. How many of us would react the way this father reacts?

And there's a lot of stuff I haven't gone into here. In the Hebrew culture of Christ's time, to ask for your inheritance early would have been seen as a complete rejection of your father. It was to wish him dead. That sin alone would be enough to have you disowned, not merely by your father, but by the whole community.

To then go to a foreign country, associate with unbelievers, engage in ungodly behavior, and become a caretaker of swine, was to add one unforgivable offense to another. And, in light of all this, for your father to be so undignified as to *run* to you, accept you back into his household as if nothing had happened, and throw a feast for you would be a complete departure from the strict norms of the culture, and would result in him being ostracized from the community as well.

I mentioned earlier that the word *prodigal* means squander, and that when it's used in a negative sense, it means "to squander or waste money or resources, to be rashly and recklessly extravagant."

But it can also be used in a positive sense, and it then means "to squander gifts, to be filled with great abundance and to be lavish in giving generously, freely, and profusely."

When the prodigal son returns home, he is met by the prodigal *father*, a father who is so full of love that he gives it out freely and in abundance, not based on merit, but on relationship: "This *son of mine* was dead and is alive again."

In this father, we see God the Father, the Father who is "Rich in Mercy," the Father who is "visible" for us in the Divine Mercy Image. He is the Prodigal Father, full of love and compassion, always watching and waiting for us to come home. There's no limit to his generosity. He is always blessing, always inviting us back into His Heart, always squandering grace, squandering love, squandering mercy.

The Elder Son

The elder son doesn't share his father's joy. He's not happy at all. Coming in from the fields and hearing the sounds of music and dancing, he asks one of the servants what is happening. The servant replies:

> Your brother has come, and your father has killed the fatted calf, because he has received him safe and sound.
>
> Lk 15:27

The elder son becomes angry and resentful, and refuses to go in. When the father hears of this, he comes out to find him (just as he had run to his younger son), and he pleads with him to come in and join them. But his son complains bitterly:

> Behold, these many years I have served you, and I never disobeyed your command; yet you never gave me a kid, that I might make merry with my friends. But when this

son of yours came, who has devoured your
living with harlots, you killed for him the
fatted calf!

Lk 15:29-30

His father responds,

Son, you are always with me, and all that
is mine is yours. But we had to celebrate and
rejoice, because this brother of yours was
dead and has come to life; he was lost and
has been found.

Lk 15:31-32 NRSV

I mentioned at the beginning of this chapter that
the elder son was also prodigal. What did *he* squander? The same thing as the younger son. No, not the
money, but his inheritance, the *real inheritance* that
neither understood and both wasted — the treasure
of their sonship, their relationship with the father.

Both sons are focused on themselves so completely
that they don't really see the father, don't understand
and value the close, loving relationship he wants to
have with them. They have a distorted view of their
father as a somehow distant authority figure whose
love and approval they have to earn.

The younger son feels he no longer "deserves" to be called a son because he has *broken all the rules*; while the elder son feels he has "earned" special treatment because he has *kept all the rules*. Both mistakenly think the father's love depends on how they behave. (They haven't learned that the Father loves backwards.)

It's All About Relationship

Look again at the father's response to the elder son: "Son, you are always with me, and all that is mine is yours." This always reminds me of God the Father's words to Jesus at the Baptism in the Jordan: "You are my beloved Son; with you I am well pleased" (Lk 3:22, NABRE).

The Father is "well pleased." What's He pleased about? Well, look at all the good stuff Jesus has done: wonderful teachings, casting out demons, amazing miracles, countless healings, even raising people from the dead! No wonder the Father's pleased, right?

Wrong! Jesus hasn't done all those things yet. This is at the very beginning of Christ's public ministry, before He's really *done* anything. So what's the Father pleased about? It's in the first part of what He says: "You are my beloved Son." That's what He's pleased about: the love *relationship* He has with His Son.

This is what the father in the parable tries to help both his sons understand: the younger son by rejoicing in his return and fathering him so tenderly in spite of his actions; and the elder son by trying to teach him the priority of relationship over behavior.

Notice the repeated emphasis on relationship in the parable. The younger son thinks he's lost his relationship with his father:

> *Father*, ... I no longer deserve to be called your *son*.

The father reaffirms their relationship by responding with joy:

> My *son* was dead and is alive.

The elder son appears to be rejecting his blood relationship with both his father and his brother. He doesn't address his father as "father," and he doesn't use the word "brother," but, instead, says:

But when *this son of yours* came …

The father gently corrects this by reaffirming the true relationships:

Son, you are always with me … your *brother* was dead …

The father had certainly been hurt by the behavior of both his sons, and in terms of strict justice could have responded very differently. But, as Pope John Paul II points out,

After all, it was his own son who was involved, and *such a relationship could never be altered or destroyed by any sort of behavior.*

Rich in Mercy, #5

Any sort of behavior? Does that mean that the father is *condoning* his son's actions? That bad behavior is *okay?* No. It means that God the Father never acts apart from His fatherhood. He sees your behavior, and it wounds Him, but His focus is not on your behavior, and it's not on Himself. It's always on you and on the relationship He longs to have with you as

His beloved son or daughter. He's always seeking what's best for you. Your sin wounds Him because it wounds you — it pulls you away from Him.

The Father knows that your behavior isn't the problem; the problem is in your heart. All sin is an expression of what's in the heart. Your heart is sick, and He wants to heal it. He knows that, once your heart is healed, your behavior will follow suit.

If there's one thing that, as a father, I want my kids to understand, that's it. I want them to know that my love for them is unconditional and forever, that there's no behavior that could ever "alter or destroy" my relationship with them as their father, nothing that they could ever do or say that could change my love for them.

The Essence of Divine Mercy

So what should we take away from all this? What does Jesus want us to learn? Pope John Paul II writes that the parable "expresses the essence" of Divine Mercy, enabling us "to understand more fully the very mystery of mercy … to understand exactly what the mercy of God consists in" (*Rich in Mercy*, #5-6).

It all centers on the Merciful Father. "The figure of the father," the Pope explains, "reveals to us God as Father." Just as the father in the parable is "faithful to his fatherhood, faithful to the love that he had always lavished on his son," so too "the 'God and Father of our Lord, Jesus Christ' is faithful to the uttermost consequences in the history of His covenant with man. ... Even if he is a prodigal, a son does not cease to be truly his father's son" (*Rich in Mercy*, #6, 14).

As St. Paul points out, even "if we are unfaithful, he remains faithful, for he cannot deny himself" (2 Tim 2:13, NAB). How is this faithfulness expressed? In love that is "transformed into mercy," love that goes "beyond the precise norms of justice," seeking *to restore all that has been lost* (*Rich in Mercy*, #5).

> This love is able to reach down to every prodigal son, to every human misery, and above all to every form of moral misery, to sin. When this happens, the person who is the object of mercy *does not feel humiliated*, but rather found again and "restored to value."
>
> *Rich in Mercy, #5*

The person who is the object of mercy *does not feel humiliated*. God forgive me for any times I may have thought I was being merciful to someone, but did it in such a way that they felt shame or humiliation as I "bestowed" my generosity upon them. God never extends mercy like that. When God extends mercy, the one who receives it does not feel humiliated but "found again and restored to value" — *restored to value*. This is the function of mercy. *Mercy restores!*

There's a beautiful promise of this in the Book of Joel. For four years in a row, all the fields have been devastated by a great army of locusts, destroying the crops and ruining the entire harvest. And then the Lord promises mercy:

> I will restore to you the years which the swarming locust has eaten.
>
> Joel 2:25, RSVCE

God the Father wants to come into our lives. He wants to break through any way that He can, so that we will open ourselves to Him and allow Him to do what He longs to do — to restore all those "fields" in our lives that the locusts have eaten.

I don't know about you, but I have fields in my life that have been pretty devastated. I think we all do. God wants to restore everything that has been lost, because (as we saw in Secret 1) all He wants to do is father us. That's all He wants — *Father, Child, Love.* He wants to restore us in His image and likeness, restore us as His children. He wants to bring us back to Him. *He wants to bring us home.*

Journey to the Father's House

A little digression. When I was teaching literature in a public high school (more years ago than I want to admit to), I was actually able to teach this parable as a perfect example of the literary form known as the Short Story. I won't go into the technical details here, but it's a perfectly constructed story, in which all the parts work together to present particular concepts or themes.

I already went into a little of that when I talked about the interplay of words of relationship (father, son, brother) used by each of the three characters. But one of my favorite themes involves the interplay of words of *movement*, with the father and the *house* of the father as the constant and central focus.

At the beginning of the parable, the younger son left his father's house and went on a *journey* to a far-off country. "When he came to himself," he decided to *return* to his father's house to work as a servant:

> "I will arise and go to my father." …
> And he arose and came to his father.

When the father saw him, he *ran* to him, welcoming him home with great joy. The elder son *drew near to the house* where the welcome home feast was in progress, but in his anger at both his father and his brother, he refused to *go in* and join the party. So, the father *came out* of the house and entreated him to come in.

God, as we saw earlier, is a pursuing God, who "goes in search of man," always inviting us to come to Him. We came from Him, and all of life is a journey back to Him.

Pope John Paul II writes:

> The whole of the Christian life is like a great *pilgrimage to the house of the Father,*

whose unconditional love for every human creature, and in particular the "prodigal son,"... we discover anew each day. ...

This pilgrimage takes place in the heart of each person. ... The sense of being on a "journey to the Father" should encourage everyone to undertake ... a journey of authentic *conversion*.

As the Third Millennium Draws Near, #49-50; emphasis original

Authentic conversion. A real change of heart, a full turning back to God. How do we get there?

Well, actually we're trying to do it together right now. We get there by discovering, or rediscovering, the Father's mercy.

Authentic knowledge of the God of mercy, the God of tender love, is a constant and inexhaustible source of conversion. ... Conversion to God *always* consists in *discovering His mercy*, that is, in discovering that love which is patient and kind as only the Creator and Father can be. ... Conversion to God is *always* the fruit of the *rediscovery of this Father, who is rich in mercy.*

Rich in Mercy, #13

And like the father in the parable. this Father is "*always waiting* for us to have recourse to Him *in every need* and always waiting for us to study His mystery: the mystery of the Father and His love" (*Rich in Mercy*, #2).

Not just *sometimes* waiting. He's *always* waiting for us to turn to Him. And not just in our times of desperation, our "big" needs, but in *every* need. His mercy is always available.

If I could be a perfect father, isn't that what I would want for my children? For them to know that I am always there, that I am always waiting for them to turn to me with anything they need?

That's the kind of father we have in God. He is the *Prodigal* Father, always waiting for us to come home, the Merciful Father who becomes visible for us in the Divine Mercy Image — so rich in mercy that He can squander it, pouring it out through the pierced Heart of Jesus as an endless fountain for all who will receive it!

$\mathcal{S}$ECRET 6

You Should Always Pray Now and Then

Eternal Life is there, in the midst of time,
wherever we come face to face with God.

Pope Benedict XVI

The last chapter ended with the image of God the Father pouring His mercy out as an endless fountain for all who will receive it. In this chapter, I want to talk about *how* we receive it, and more specifically, how we receive it through the particular prayers and devotional practices found in the *Diary* of St. Faustina.

The Elements of the Devotion

These prayers and devotions are often referred to as the "elements of the devotion," or "vessels of mercy." The list commonly includes the Divine Mercy Image, the Hour of Mercy, the Chaplet of Divine Mercy, the Feast of Mercy, and the Novena to Divine Mercy. (I also like to include the Eucharist and Confession as "vessels of mercy," because of the special emphasis they are given in the *Diary*.)

Why a new set of prayers and devotions? From His teachings and instructions to Faustina, the Lord obviously considers them important. And they've also become important to people all over the world because of the powerful fruits that so many have experienced in their lives. What's the big deal? What makes them so special, so powerful?

The Power Is in the Passion

Grace, of course. Everything depends on grace. But, more specifically, the grace that comes from focusing on the Passion of Christ. And, as we'll see shortly, all these elements help us to recall and enter into the mystery of the Passion.

The Passion of Christ is so powerful! As Jesus told St. Faustina,

> **I give great graces to souls who meditate devoutly on My Passion. ... There is more merit to one hour of meditation on My sorrowful Passion than there is to a whole year of flagellation that draws blood.**
>
> *Diary*, 737, 369

And Faustina writes,

> Jesus told me that I please Him best by meditating on His sorrowful Passion, and by such meditation much light falls upon my soul. ... I get a clear understanding of many things I could not comprehend before.
>
> *Diary*, 267

Why is meditation on the Passion so powerful? Because the Passion is not just an historic event locked in the past. The *Catechism* teaches that Christ's

Suffering, Death, Resurrection, and Ascension form one unique event, known as the Paschal mystery. It is the one historical event that never ends and is not limited to one time or place, but is made present in all:

> The Paschal mystery ... cannot remain only in the past ... all that Christ is — *all that He did and suffered* for all men — participates in the divine eternity, and so *transcends all times while being made present in them all.*
>
> #1085; emphasis added

All that Christ "did and suffered" for us — and all the fruits He won for us — are eternal and are always available to us in every *now* moment of our lives. This last point is so important that, before we go any further, we need to take some time to talk about time.

No Time for God

Which brings us to the title of this secret. How can we *always* pray *now and then?* Well, it's another pun. By "now and then," I don't mean *occasionally*. I mean we need to pray constantly (see 1 Thes 5:17), offering our prayer both *now* (in this present moment), and also *then* (in the past).

What's that all about? The "Eternal Now" — the reality that God is not limited by time as we are. He doesn't experience events in sequence, moment by moment. He doesn't have to try to remember the past, or speculate about the future.

Perhaps a visual image would help. Imagine a timeline — a long timeline, showing all the events that *have* happened or *will* happen, from the beginning of time to the end of time.

Now, imagine God outside of all that, looking at it. He sees it all at once — past, present, and future simultaneously. Everything is *now* to God. He lives in the *Eternal Now*.

So, what does that mean for you and me? The *Catechism* makes it really clear:

> Jesus knew and loved us *each* and all during his life, his agony and his Passion, and gave himself up for *each one* of us.
>
> #478; emphasis added

The Passion of Christ is personal! Christ didn't just die for *humanity*, He died for *you*, personally. He saw you, two thousand years ago, from the Cross, loved you, pulled all your sin into His body, and died for you.

If you had been the only person who needed to be saved, He would have died *just for you*. He died "once for all" (Heb 10:10) — all people and all sin. He died *then* for sins you haven't even committed yet.

Pope John Paul II refers to this as *"a mysterious 'oneness of time,'"* whereby what Christ did *then* affects us *now*; and what we do *now* affected Him *then* (*The Church of the Eucharist*, #5).

Okay, so with all this in mind, let's take a look at each of the elements of the Divine Mercy devotion. I'm not going to make any attempt to give a complete explanation of any of these — that would take many books, not just a chapter.

Let's just look at how each allows us to pray *now* and *then*, and how they fit in with each other and the truths we've already seen. (If you want to go deeper — and I encourage that — there's a list of additional resources in the back of the book.)

The Metaphor of the Fountain

I mentioned earlier that the elements of the devotion are also known as "vessels of mercy." As we've already seen, one of the metaphors most often used to represent the outpouring of mercy is that of the fountain — a metaphor that is used constantly throughout the *Diary*.

If you want to draw water from a fountain, you need a vessel to put it in — a little glass, a bowl, a pail, or a huge bucket. The larger the vessel, the more water you can carry.

The "vessels of mercy" all allow us to draw grace from the fountain of mercy. They also have several things in common: they are dependent upon trust; they reflect and point to the Eucharist; they open us to receive the Father's mercy; and they enable us to *enter into the Passion of Christ* in such a way that it's as if we have stepped out of time and into eternity.

The Necessity of Trust

I said that the vessels of mercy are all dependent

upon trust. It's actually much more than that. In one sense, the *only* vessel is trust. All the prayers and devotions that we'll be talking about are vessels of mercy only to the extent that they express and manifest trust:

> **The graces of My mercy are drawn by means of *one vessel only*, and that is — trust. The more a soul trusts, the more it will receive.**
>
> *Diary*, 1578

Trust is at the heart of the message of mercy. Everything we do, every prayer we say, must be fueled by trust.

The Divine Mercy Image

The Divine Mercy Image is a perfect example of Christ's insistence on trust. When Christ spoke to St. Faustina about the Image, He referred to it as a vessel of grace, but emphasized the signature of trust, without which the Image would be incomplete:

> I am offering people a vessel with which
> they are to keep coming for graces to the
> fountain of mercy. That vessel is this image
> with the signature: "Jesus, I trust in You."
>
> *Diary*, 327

Fr. Ignacy Rozycki, the theologian who did a ten-year study of St. Faustina's writings as part of the Vatican's official investigation for her Cause, writes that Christ's promise to "grant unimaginable graces to those who trust" in His mercy, refers "first of all" to the veneration of the Image. And he adds that Christ did not place "any limits" to the graces we can receive through venerating this Image "with unwavering trust."

As we saw in Secret 3, the Image is a complete, visual "Theology of Divine Mercy" and a powerful icon of the Paschal Mystery. The more we gaze on the Image, the more we are drawn into that mystery. Our gazing is itself a meditation on the Passion.

We are transported back in time to the Cross. We are there and, seeing the "proof" of His mercy — the torture He endured out of love for us, the terrible price He willingly paid for our sins — we are led to respond to Him with gratitude and trust.

Face to face with the personal consequences of our sins, the reality that our sins added to His pain, we also experience the "tears of repentance" that convert our hearts and lead us to amend our lives (see *Catechism*, #1429, 1431-1432).

After reading Secret 3, you should now be an expert on the Image, so I'm not going to say any more about it here — except to give you two things to keep in mind as we go along.

First, as the central feature of the Divine Mercy devotion, the Image is intimately linked with each of the other elements we'll be talking about.

Second, and perhaps most significantly, it is also a representation of what we would see if we could look "beyond the veil" of the Eucharist. (We'll see more about that in Secret 7.)

The Hour of Mercy

In His revelations to St. Faustina, Christ made it clear that, every afternoon, when we hear the clock strike three, He wants us to take at least a moment, from the busy *now* of our day, to focus on His Passion and Death in the *then* moment of His great agony.

Why? Because "at that moment, mercy was opened wide" for us. It is the "hour of great mercy, … the hour of grace for the whole world," the hour when "mercy triumphed over justice" (*Diary*, 1320, 1572).

Specifically, what does He ask us to do?

> To implore His mercy for the whole world, especially for sinners;

> To immerse ourselves in His Passion, especially in His abandonment "at the moment of agony";

> To immerse ourselves completely in His mercy, "adoring and glorifying it."
>
> *Diary*, 1320, 1572

How does He want us to do this? Well, He tells us what He wants, but then, in a sense, He "has mercy on us," and keeps asking for less and less.

I have to smile a little when I think of this, remembering how much Fr. Kosicki loved this section of the *Diary* and referred to it as "God reversing the roles." It always made him think of the famous exchange between Abraham and God just before the destruction of Sodom and Gomorrah.

Abraham, concerned that the righteous will be destroyed along with the wicked, asks God to spare the cities if He finds fifty good people. The Lord agrees, and Abraham begins to "bargain" with God — almost like an auctioneer in reverse:

> "Okay, how about 45, Lord? Will you let them go for 45? ... How about 40? Do I hear 40? ... Now 30? ... 20? ... 10, Lord? Will you spare them for 10?"
>
> See Gen 18:16-32

But when the Lord speaks to St. Faustina about how He wants us to pray at the hour of mercy, she doesn't have to bargain. Again, it helps me to envision this as a personal, down-to-earth conversation, so pardon me for another rather loose paraphrase (and feel free to insert your own name):

> Okay, Vinny, what I really want you to do at three o'clock is to try to *make the Stations of the Cross.*

But, if you're not able to do that, at least *take a minute to go into the church* and spend a moment *adoring my merciful Heart in the Blessed Sacrament*. ...

Or, if you can't do that, then just *stop whatever you're doing* — even for just a moment — and *immerse yourself in prayer*.
See *Diary*, 1572

Why is God willing to accept so little from us? Because the Paschal Mystery never ends, remember? Christ is forever offering Himself to the Father for the sake of souls. He *wants* to have mercy on all. And He wants us to share that desire, to unite ourselves with Him, in whatever big or little ways we can.

The promises He makes for those of us willing to do even the minimum in this hour of mercy, to step out of time and join Him in His eternal offering, make this so clear:

I will allow you to *enter into* My mortal sorrow. In this hour, I will refuse nothing to the soul that makes a request of Me

in virtue of My Passion. ...

In this hour you can obtain everything for yourself and for others.

Diary, 1320, 1572

The Chaplet of Divine Mercy

The Chaplet of Divine Mercy — because it is so completely focused on the Passion of Christ — has become the prayer most often prayed at three o'clock. Many people actually seem to think that they *have* to pray it at three, and some seem to think that it's the *only* time they should pray it.

Neither thought is accurate. It is certainly appropriate to pray the Chaplet at three, but the Lord never asked for it to be prayed at that time. What He asked was for it to be prayed all the time. He told St. Faustina to pray it "unceasingly" and to encourage others to pray it as well (see *Diary,* 687, 1541).

He spoke to her about the Chaplet many times, often giving her specific times and ways to pray it, along with particular intentions.

Novena of Chaplets

The morning after she received the words of the Chaplet, the Lord told her to recite it immediately every time she entered the chapel (see *Diary*, 476). He then told her to recite it for nine days. He repeated this request for a novena of Chaplets at other times as well, once telling her to ask her superior to have all the sisters pray this novena (714); another time telling her to pray it on the nine days preceeding the Feast of Mercy (796).

> **By this novena [of Chaplets], I will grant every possible grace for souls.**
>
> *Diary,* 796

Instructed and inspired by the Lord, Faustina prayed the Chaplet over and over again, in all kinds of situations, and for a wide variety of intentions. Her main intention was always for mercy on the whole world, but for many other intentions as well. She prayed for God's mercy to hold back His just punishment; she prayed for the conversion of individual sinners, for priests, for the dying, for her country, and even for changes in the weather conditions.

(This novena of Chaplets should not be confused with the special Novena to Divine Mercy that the Lord also asked St. Faustina to say in preparation for the Feast. We'll see more about this later.)

Power to Spare

From the moment He gave her the words of the Chaplet, the Lord made it clear to Faustina that this prayer, when prayed from the heart with trust, would have great power and would draw "unimaginable graces" (*Diary*, 687).

Recalling that moment in her *Diary*, she explains that she saw an angel about to destroy a certain city. She started begging the angel to wait, so that the people would repent, but realized that her prayer "was a mere nothing in the face of the divine anger" (474).

Suddenly she "saw the Most Holy Trinity," felt the "power of Jesus' grace," and was immediately "snatched up before the Throne of God" (474).

Wow! When God decides to reveal a powerful prayer to us, even the best Hollywood producers couldn't make it any more dramatic!

Faustina then began to pray again, but this time with the words of the Chaplet, which she "heard interiorly" (474). As she prayed, the angel became helpless and "could not carry out the just punishment which was rightly due for sins":

> Never before had I prayed with such inner power as I did then.
>
> *Diary*, 474

Over time, she realized that sometimes the result of praying the Chaplet would be immediate; and, at other times, she would have to persevere in prayer. But it was always extremely powerful.

Two different weather-related occasions provide a perfect example. She was awakened one night by a terrible storm and began to pray that it wouldn't do any harm. The Lord told her to say the Chaplet for the storm to stop. She recalls,

> I began immediately to say the chaplet, and hadn't even finished it when the storm suddenly ceased.
>
> *Diary*, 1731

On another occasion, in a time of drought and intense heat, she resolved to pray the Chaplet until the Lord sent rain. She prayed non-stop for three hours, at which point "the sky covered over with clouds, and a heavy rain fell on the earth" (1128).

From these and many other answered prayers, Faustina came to realize "that this prayer was pleasing to God, and that this chaplet was most powerful (1791). ... The Lord let me know that everything can be obtained by means of this prayer" (1128).

Promises for the Chaplet

The Lord gave several, very specific promises for those who would pray the Chaplet with complete trust in accordance with His will:

> **Oh, what great graces I will grant to souls who say this chaplet.**
>
> *Diary,* 848

> **The souls that say this chaplet will be embraced by My mercy during their lifetime and especially at the hour of their death.**
>
> *Diary,* 754

When hardened sinners say it, I will fill their souls with peace, and the hour of their death will be a happy one. ... Even if there were a sinner most hardened, if he were to recite this chaplet only once, he would receive grace from My infinite mercy.

Diary, 1541, 687

When they say this chaplet in the presence of the dying, I will stand between My Father and the dying person, not as the just Judge but as the merciful Savior.

Diary, 1541

Through the chaplet you will obtain everything, if what you ask for is compatible with My will.

Diary, 1731

To understand why the Lord gave us this prayer and why He promises such an abundance of grace for those who pray it, let's look at the words of the two main parts of the prayer itself.

Eternal Father, I offer You the Body and Blood, Soul and Divinity of Your dearly beloved Son, Our Lord Jesus Christ, in atonement for our sins and those of the whole world.

For the sake of His sorrowful Passion have mercy on us and on the whole world.

Diary, 476

"Eternal Father"

Eternal Father. The Chaplet is a prayer — and an offering — to the *Father.* Our focus is on Christ's Passion and Death on the Cross, but we're *talking to God the Father* as Jesus, Himself, did ("Father, forgive them ... Father, into your hands ..."). As Pope John Paul II writes,

> The cross ... speaks and never ceases to speak of God the Father, who is absolutely faithful to His eternal love for man, since He "so loved the world" ... that "he gave his only Son." ... Believing in the crucified Son means "seeing the Father."
>
> *Rich in Mercy*, #7

Christ ... addresses Himself to the

Father — that Father whose love He has preached to people, to whose mercy He has borne witness through all of His activity. But He is not spared ... the terrible suffering of death on the cross: For our sake "God made him to be sin who knew no sin."

Rich in Mercy, #7

He is not spared. People call out, "He saved others; let him save himself if he is the Messiah of God" (Lk 23:35, NIV). But He, who could have asked the Father for this, does not. Embracing the Cross, He offers Himself *in our place,* in atonement for *our sins,* and thus "renders full justice" to the Father and fulfills the Father's plan of mercy (*Rich in Mercy*, #7).

In a sense, Christ, in complete union with the Eternal Father, *denies Himself mercy so that we might receive mercy.* Through His Cross and Resurrection, we gain "access ... to the Father" and His love (Eph 2:18).

Christ, whom the Father "did not spare" for the sake of man, and who in His passion and in the torment of the cross did not obtain human mercy, has revealed in His resurrection the fullness of the love that the

171

Father has for Him and, in Him, for all
people.

Rich in Mercy, # 8

"I offer You the Body and Blood, Soul and Divinity of Your dearly beloved Son" …

Body and Blood, Soul and Divinity. Ever hear these words before? This is, word-for-word, the Council of Trent definition of the Eucharist. It is also the phrase used by the angel at Fatima when he prostrated himself before the Blessed Sacrament.

As Fr. Kosicki expressed it, the Chaplet is like a "Mini-Mass: an extension of the Eucharist to each moment." We are offering Christ Himself — His entire humanity together with His Divine Person.

By this offering, we are simultaneously uniting ourselves with Christ's sacrifice on the Cross two thousand years ago, with His Eucharistic presence *now* in all the tabernacles of the world, and with His eternal presence in Heaven, where He perpetually offers His once-for-all sacrifice to the Father.

A Double Offering

To fully understand the offering we make through the Chaplet, it helps to look at what we do during the Mass. At every celebration of the Mass, you and I are each called to make a double offering: to offer *Christ* (the sacrificial Victim) with the priest, and to *offer ourselves through Christ*.

As the Second Vatican Council teaches us, we should not attend Mass "as strangers or silent spectators" but should "*take part* in the sacred action ... with devotion and *full collaboration*, ... offering the Immaculate Victim ... through the hands of the priest," and *also offering ourselves* "through Christ the Mediator" (*Constitution on the Sacred Liturgy*, #48).

I, not *We* — for *Us*, not *Me*

"Eternal Father, *I* offer ..." Sometimes, when people pray the Chaplet together, they change *I* offer to *we* offer. But this negates part of what this prayer is all about. There's a little rhyme that helps me remember this: *I, not we — for us, not me.*

You can offer *yourself* to Jesus; you can unite *your-*

self with Him and His offering. But you can't do that in proxy for me. I have to choose to do that myself. You can't offer *my* "stuff."

Let's look at a couple of similar examples: "Jesus, I trust in You." *You* can't make a commitment to Jesus that *I'm* going to trust Him. That's a decision and a commitment that only *I* can make. And, at Easter, when we're asked, at the renewal of our baptismal promises, "Do you reject Satan?" we don't all respond, *"We do."* We *each* respond, *"I* do."

In the same way, when we pray the Chaplet, the offering we each make is individual and personal — I, not we.

But even though I, myself, *make* the offering, I'm not making it *for myself.* I'm not offering it for *me*; I'm offering it for *us.*

Christ's offering on the Cross wasn't for Himself: it was a "once for all" offering (Heb 10:10) — for all sin and all people. So, when I unite myself with His offering, it's not a selfish offering. It's an offering that I make with Jesus "in atonement for *our* sins" (my sins and the sins of those I love, those who are with me, or those I'm praying for).

I then extend that offering to also include everyone else — "and those of *the whole world*." And I do the same thing in the plea for mercy that follows: "Have mercy on *us* and on *the whole world*."

The Chaplet should never be a selfish prayer. Yes, of course, we can include our own personal intentions. We already saw that Faustina prayed the Chaplet for all kinds of different intentions — even the weather! But the main intention must always be Christ's main intention, in union with the Father's plan (and great desire) to "have mercy upon all" (Rom 11:32). For it is no part of the Father's plan that even one of us should be lost (see Mt 18:14).

"In Atonement ..."

But how can I offer Christ? Who am I to presume that I can offer Christ's sacrifice to the Father? Who am I to think that there could be any real value in joining my offering of myself to His? How can I add anything to His perfect offering?

For me the answer has to do with understanding what the word *atonement* really means. The phrase used in the Chaplet is an echo of St. John's teaching that Christ "is the atoning sacrifice for our sins, and not only for ours but also for the sins of the whole world" (1 Jn 2:2, NIV).

This sacrifice wasn't forced on Christ, and He didn't make it reluctantly. He offered Himself freely "in atonement" for our sins. That doesn't mean that he merely "made up for" or "compensated for" our sins. It means that He did it *in complete union* with the Father, who, in Christ, "was reconciling the world [reuniting us] to himself" (2 Cor, 5:19). Christ's "atonement" was "*at-one-ment*" with the Father.

Through the Chaplet we say a complete "yes" to Christ's complete "yes" to the Father. We unite ourselves with Him in His offering, His "at-one-ment" with the Father. And we also gather all our own sufferings, weaknesses, problems, anxieties — all that's a part of who we are — and offer it to the Father, in union with Christ's perfect offering.

Solidarity with Christ

Our best model for this, of course, is Our Lady.

Standing at the foot of the Cross, she offered herself in faithful solidarity with Him, sharing His suffering so completely that, as Simeon had prophesied, her heart, too, was pierced (see Lk 2:35). And, in spite of how much it must have hurt this mother to see her Son so tortured and mutilated, she willed to join Him in His self-emptying "yes" to the Father:

> The Blessed Virgin ... faithfully persevered in her union with her Son unto the Cross, where she stood, in keeping with the divine plan, grieving exceedingly with her only begotten Son, uniting herself with a maternal heart with His sacrifice, and lovingly consenting to the immolation of this Victim which she herself had brought forth.
>
> *Lumen Gentium*, #58

God's Thirst for Souls

In this union of our offering with Christ's, what we're doing is taking on His thirst for souls — which is simply the Father's thirst to restore to His embrace the children whom He so lovingly created.

We need to realize that when we offer the Chaplet, we are taking on all the souls of the world. We're taking them into our embrace, too. We are thirsting for their salvation as Christ did.

Christ pleaded with Faustina to help Him save souls by joining her sufferings to His:

> During Holy Mass, I saw the Lord Jesus nailed upon the cross amidst great torments. A soft moan issued from His Heart. After some time, He said, **I thirst. I thirst for the salvation of souls. Help Me, My daughter, to save souls. Join your sufferings to My Passion and offer them to the heavenly Father for sinners.**
>
> *Diary,* 1032

Faustina responded to this so completely that she became, in essence, a *living Chaplet:*

> It is my constant endeavor to plead for mercy for the world. I unite myself closely with Jesus and stand before Him *as an atoning sacrifice on behalf of the world.* God will refuse me nothing when I entreat Him with the voice of His Son. My sacrifice is

nothing in itself, but when I join it to the sacrifice of Jesus Christ, it becomes all-powerful and has the power to appease divine wrath.

Diary, 482

The Cross, the Image, and the Tabernacle

My favorite place to pray the Chaplet is in Adoration before the Blessed Sacrament. When I can't actually do this, I unite myself with the Lord's Eucharistic presence and gaze in spirit on the Cross, the Image, and the tabernacle, with the rays of mercy streaming from each, like a triple-exposure photograph. To me, it's all one.

When I'm praying alone, I often pause and add a few "thought words" that go along with those mental images. (I'm not suggesting that you do this — just putting it out there as a helpful meditation):

"Eternal Father, I offer You the Body and Blood, Soul and Divinity of Your dearly beloved Son, Our Lord Jesus Christ, …" *(on the Cross then, and in all the tabernacles of the world now)* …

Somehow this ties everything together for me and helps make my offering more real.

"For the sake of His sorrowful Passion"

When I was first introduced to the Chaplet, I just didn't "get" this phrase. What did it mean? Was I asking God to have mercy *because* of Christ's Passion, based on the *merits* of His Passion? Or was I asking Him to have mercy on us *for His Son's sake?*

Fr. Rozycki explains that we are not appealing "to the satisfaction which Jesus offered for our sins," but rather to the merciful love of the Father and the Son for us — *"that love which found its highest expression in the sorrowful Passion of Jesus.* In other words, we turn to the strongest motive in order to be heard by God."

What we are really praying, he continues, is that "so much hardship, so much suffering not be in vain. … the same idea which Thomas of Celano expressed in the hymn *Dies Irae*:"

> Exhausted You sought me,
> crucified You saved me,
> may Your Wounds not be in vain.

When I read that, it all finally made sense to me, and I was moved to tears. Now, every time my mouth prays, "For the sake of His sorrowful Passion …," my heart is pleading, "Father, please … Let His sufferings not have been in vain!"

A Matter of Life and Death

Before we move on, I want to briefly mention two specific intentions for which the Chaplet has become known as an exceptionally powerful form of intercessory prayer — for the unborn and for the dying.

Remember the avenging angel who was about to destroy a city, but was prevented from doing so when Faustina first began praying the Chaplet? She didn't identify the city or the sin in her *Diary*, but Blessed Fr. Sopocko, her spiritual director, later revealed that the city was Warsaw and the sin was abortion.

St. Faustina records in her *Diary* that, on at least three occasions, the Lord allowed her to suffer extremely violent pain for three hours in "reparation to God for the souls murdered in the wombs," and she accepted this agony with submission, saying, "If only I could save even one soul from murder by means of these sufferings!" (*Diary*, 1276).

For this reason, the Chaplet has become, for many, a prayer for life — for unborn children, and for those who have had, or plan to have, an abortion; and it is often prayed by people keeping vigil outside abortion clinics.

It has also become widely known and used as a prayer for the dying, because of Faustina's own example and the clear desire of the Lord:

> **At the hour of their death, I defend as My own glory every soul that will say this chaplet; or when others say it for a dying person, the indulgence is the same.**
>
> *Diary*, 811

> **When they say this chaplet in the presence of the dying, I will stand between My Father and the dying person, not as the just Judge but as the merciful Savior.**
>
> *Diary*, 1541

In the year 2000, Pope John Paul II recognized and affirmed the value of this form of prayer by imparting a special Apostolic Blessing for all those who, during Eucharistic Adoration, would pray the Chaplet for the sick and dying.

The Feast of Mercy

In discussing the Feast of Mercy, now also known as "Divine Mercy Sunday," or simply "Mercy Sunday," I don't feel any need to give all the details. Much has been written about this Feast, and a great deal of information is readily available.

I'll briefly summarize the basic details, but then I want to share some thoughts about some of the things I feel are most important, and that even many people who participate in the Feast every year may not realize.

So, here we go with some basic "Feast Facts":

† Faustina didn't "invent" this Feast. Christ repeatedly insisted on it, mentioning it fourteen times in the *Diary*;

† The Feast is to be observed on the Second Sunday of Easter (which, in the

year 2000, Pope John Paul II renamed "Divine Mercy Sunday");

† The Divine Mercy Image is to be blessed and publically venerated;

† The homily is to be preached on Divine Mercy, especially the "unimaginable Mercy" that the Father pours upon us through Christ's "human Heart, above all attested to by His Passion";

† Our observance of the Feast must include acts of mercy for others, by word, deed, or prayer;

† The graces we receive on this day (as on every day) will be directly proportionate to the degree of trust we place in Jesus;

† To fully receive the great promises of Jesus for this day, we must sincerely repent of our sins and be in a state of grace through sacramental Confession; and we must receive Holy Communion worthily on that day itself;

† The Feast is to prepare the world for Christ's second coming, a "last hope of salvation" for sinners, a "Day of Mercy" before the "Day of Justice" (*Diary*, 429, 965, 1588);

† The Feast is to be preceded by a Novena. (For us, this means the Novena of Chaplets, as we've already seen, though we may also pray the special Novena given to St. Faustina, which we'll see later.)

The Feast of the Prodigal Father

Okay, that's done. (But remember, that's just a summary; there's a lot more information available about all of that.) Now we can move on to the heart of it all.

I want to bring you back to one word: *squander.* To me, more than anything else, the Feast of Mercy is the "Feast of the Prodigal Father" — the day when, for the sake of His Son's sorrowful Passion, the Father lets out all the stops, opening up all the floodgates of the ocean of mercy, and pouring out the fruits of Christ's sacrifice on everyone.

The Feast of Mercy is the celebration of God the Father *squandering grace*, providing a refuge for all, a last opportunity to turn to Him so that, indeed, all Christ's suffering will not have been in vain, but will allow the Father's plan of mercy for all to be fulfilled.

Not a Magic Wand

Because the Lord promised an extraordinary grace of complete forgiveness of sins *and* punishment for anyone who goes to Confession and who receives Communion on Mercy Sunday, many people seem to focus all their attention on getting that grace, often waiting for hours in Confession lines and making sure they receive Communion — as if the outward observance of those requirements is all that matters.

Yes, it's a great promise. But it's not a magic wand! We receive grace — always — in proportion to what's going on in our hearts and minds. *We need to prepare for Mercy Sunday in our hearts!* Our motive for receiving the sacraments should never be simply to "get" something for ourselves, to "get" the special graces promised; but rather to "give" ourselves to the Lord more completely — to prepare ourselves to receive these graces *worthily* through *real repentance, real trust, real openness to changing our lives!*

Cardinal Francis Macharski, Archbishop of St. Faustina's archdiocese of Krakow, Poland, stressed that this preparation should be going on all during

Lent, and that we should not put off our Confession until Mercy Sunday. It's not necessary to go to Confession on Mercy Sunday itself; to receive the special graces promised by the Lord, we simply need to be in a state of grace through sacramental Confession and to receive Communion worthily on that day with trust in Divine Mercy.

St. Faustina, herself, didn't go to Confession on Mercy Sunday; she went on the day before (see *Diary*, 1072). And Cardinal Macharski urges people to go even before Holy Week, so that they will be in a state of grace throughout the Triduum and the feasts of Easter Sunday and Mercy Sunday.

As Dr. Robert Stackpole explains:

> Sin without repentance is the only obstacle that prevents Jesus Christ from deeply healing and sanctifying our souls on these great feast days. That's why it is best not to count the days before these feasts and try to abide by some minimum requirement about when to make your confession.
>
> Rather, take an inventory of your heart. If there is anything in your heart that is

impeding your love for Jesus and His for you — any grudge still held, any despair or mistrust, any kind word left unsaid, any duty seriously neglected — this is the time for a "spring cleaning of the soul." Make a good confession, and then try your best, with the help of grace, to keep your soul clean, open, and ready to receive our Savior in Holy Communion on the first and second Sundays of Easter.

Why Eucharist and Confession?

As we go through this "spring cleaning," we would do well to also think about why the Lord has made the special graces of this feast contingent upon the worthy reception of the Sacraments of Reconciliation and Eucharist.

Clearly He seems to be emphasizing here (as He does throughout the *Diary* of St. Faustina) that these sacraments are, in a special way, sacraments of mercy, and they are intimately linked together. Receiving them — any time, but especially in observance of the Feast of Mercy — we are receiving the Fountain of

Life, the Fountain of Mercy.

One of the things that links them together is their connection to the Passion of Christ in the Eternal Now. Through these two sacraments, all the graces of mercy gushing from His pierced Heart are available to us at each *now* moment of our lives.

Every time you walk up the aisle to receive the Eucharist, in whatever church, at whatever time, you are at the foot of the Cross with Mary and John, and the blood and water from Christ's Heart is pouring out upon you. As Pope John Paul II teaches, through this "oneness of time," all the fruits of Christ's Sacrifice are "'concentrated' forever in the gift of the Eucharist" and are applied to you now as you receive (*The Church of the Eucharist*, 5, 12).

The same thing happens in Confession. Time and space disappear and you are *at* Calvary. Christ isn't forgiving you *now* in the confessional. He forgave you two thousand years ago. You're simply receiving it now.

As our Lord revealed to St. Faustina:

When you go to confession, to this fountain of My mercy, the Blood and Water

**which came forth from My Heart always
flows down upon your soul and ennobles it.**

Diary, 1602

There's a lot more to this — I've only just skimmed the surface here to give you a sense of how the Eternal Now applies to our reception of these sacraments. If you'd like to go deeper, there's much more in chapter 3 of *7 Secrets of the Eucharist* ("There Is Only One Mass") and in chapter 5 of *7 Secrets of Confession* ("You've Got Mail!").

No Limit to the Graces of This Feast

As great as it is, the special grace of complete forgiveness and punishment that God offers us on this Feast is not the only grace He wants to give. Sometimes we expect too little; we ask for too little. God wants to *squander* grace, remember? There's no limit to the graces He wants to give us on that day. As Fr. Rozycki explains,

> The very depths of Jesus' generosity are opened on this day in order to pour out upon souls, without any holding back, *graces*

> *of every type and every degree — even the most unheard of.* This generosity is ... the motive for calling upon The Divine Mercy with great and limitless trust, for *all the gifts of grace* that Our Lord *wants to squander* on this Sunday.

To receive this "extraordinary abundance of graces," Fr. Rozycki continues, we must "approach His Mercy with the greatest trust possible." As Jesus, Himself, told Faustina,

> **I desire to grant *unimaginable graces* to those souls who trust in My mercy.**
>
> *Diary*, 687

Graces of every type and every degree? ... even the most unheard of? ... unimaginable graces? Are you serious? I don't know about you, but I've heard about a lot of "amazing grace," and I can easily imagine some pretty awesome things. God wants to give me graces that I can't even *imagine?* Well, sign me up! I'm there, Lord. Lay it on me.

Greedy for Grace

Like the Eucharist (which, as we've seen, is an integral part of this day), the Feast of Mercy is an "all you can eat" banquet. No fixed menu here with small portions served. It's an endless buffet, and there's no limit to what you can have. It all depends on your appetite and the size of your plate. And the plate is trust. The larger your plate, the more you can take; the greater your trust, the more you receive. God has more to give you than you can possibly take in.

Sometimes we don't ask enough of God; we don't expect enough. We're content with the "same old, same old." Christ told Faustina that it *delights Him* when we appeal to His Mercy, and He urged her to take as many "treasures" of His Heart as she could carry — for herself and others (*Diary*, 294).

Wanting more and more of something is not typically a good thing, but *it's always okay to want more of God*. It's okay to be greedy for grace, *especially on this Feast*. Don't come, like the prodigal son, expecting to be treated like a hired hand; come as a child to receive your inheritance from the Father who wants to give you more than you can even imagine!

When you come to this Feast, bring all your intentions, all your needs, all your desires, all your loved ones in your heart. Ask Him to give you more than He's ever given you before, to fill you with more of Himself, to heal all that's broken in you, to do all that He, in His love, longs to do for you — and ask Him to help you trust more and more in His endless mercy.

> From the depths of the mystery of God, the great river of mercy wells up and overflows unceasingly.
>
> *Face of Mercy*, #25

The Novena to Divine Mercy

I mentioned earlier that on at least one occasion, the Lord asked St. Faustina to pray a novena of Chaplets, beginning on Good Friday and ending on the eve of the Feast of Divine Mercy (see *Diary*, 796). He also gave her a second novena, with special prayers to say each day in preparation for the Feast;

and this has now become known as the Novena to Divine Mercy (see *Diary*, 1209-1229).

Unlike the novena of Chaplets, which the Lord wanted everyone to pray (not only in preparation for the Feast, but constantly), this Novena seems to have been given to Faustina primarily for her own use as part of her mission as a chosen soul, both on earth and in Heaven. And the Lord made amazing promises for the souls that she would bring to Him:

> **On each day you will bring to My Heart a different group of souls, and you will immerse them in this ocean of My mercy, and *I will bring all these souls into the house of My Father*. You will do this in this life and in the next. *I will deny nothing to any soul whom you will bring to the fount of My mercy*.**
>
> *Diary*, 1209

Wow! Faustina, please be sure to include me when you pray this Novena!

Though the Lord never specifically told Faustina to encourage others to pray this Novena, the entire Novena is included in the *Diary*, so He seems to have wanted it to be available to everyone, and it has become increasingly popular throughout the world.

Many people, when they pray this Novena, also include the Chaplet in fulfillment of the Lord's specific request for a novena of Chaplets.

Each day of the Novena is like a symphony of prayer in three movements, with certain phrases recurring throughout. The first begins with "Today bring to Me ..." as Christ describes a particular group of souls and asks Faustina to "immerse them" in His mercy. (This always brings me back to the Divine Mercy Image, with that left hand, inviting us to come to Him, entering into the very depths of His merciful Heart.)

Then comes a prayer composed by Faustina, asking the "Most Merciful Jesus" to receive these souls into the "abode" of His "Most Compassionate Heart" — which always makes me think of the tabernacle, where the Eucharistic Heart of Jesus beats for us.

This is followed by Faustina's prayer to the Father: "Eternal Father, turn Your merciful gaze upon ... ." Her prayers for each day are like songs of trust in the Father's love, asking that these souls may come to glorify His great mercy.

Many of the daily intentions that Christ gave her show how personally what we do *now* affected Christ *then*. Notice especially the verb tenses:

> Today bring to Me the souls of priests and religious ... It *was* they who *gave* Me the strength to endure My bitter Passion.
>
> *Diary*, 1212

> Today bring to me all devout and faithful souls. ... These souls *brought* me consolation on the Way of the Cross. They *were* that drop of consolation in the midst of an ocean of bitterness.
>
> *Diary*, 1214

> Today bring to Me the pagans and those who do not yet know me. I *was* thinking also of them during My bitter Passion, and their *future* zeal *comforted* My Heart.
>
> *Diary*, 1216

The Novena shows us that our involvement with the Passion of Christ is *real!* And it's *personal.* Whether we're aware of it or not, everything you and

I do now affected Him then. It either comforted and consoled Him or made His suffering worse. In every *now* of my life, I hurt or help in the *then* of His agony.

One "Final" Thing

There's one more reality that's important — and consoling — to understand about the Eternal Now of God: what you *pray* now, he *heard* then.

My brother Art died of a massive heart attack. When I heard that he had been taken to the hospital, I began to pray the Chaplet for him. But I later found out that he had died almost immediately. My prayer was too late.

But it *wasn't* too late. As I wrote in *21 Ways to Worship,*

> It's never too late to pray, because God is not subject to time. He knows all things, all possibilities, past, present, and future. He knew about my prayer for Art even before either of us was born, and I firmly believe that He was with Art in a special way during the moments before He died, in answer to the prayer I hadn't prayed yet.

When I finally realized this reality of the timelessness of prayer, I found myself thinking back on an earlier, similar tragedy — the death of my dad.

I was 19 and sound asleep when he suffered a heart attack at home. When I was awakened, he was already dead, and I was so devastated that I'm not sure whether I prayed at all. But it doesn't matter; I can pray for him right now, fifty years later:

> *"Lord, let it be that You were with him then, that in those final instants You were there to flood him with grace. I ask You now, Lord, to let the blood and water that gushed forth from Your Heart, pour upon him then, inviting him to whatever deeper conversion he may have needed to bring him to You. Jesus, I trust in You."*

We need to really understand God's thirst for souls! He loves my brother and my dad more than I ever could. He chose each of them to be His sons. He formed them in their mothers' wombs. He pursued them with His love in countless ways all through their lives. How could I doubt that He would be with them in their final moments, doing whatever possible (short of forcing them) to bring them to Himself? It's unthinkable. It would be a complete contradiction to His love, to who He is.

God never gives up on us, but continuously offers us the grace of conversion. Even at the last moment of our lives, God, in His great mercy, offers us what St. Faustina calls "final grace" — a special illumination of the soul that presents us with a final choice to accept or reject Him.

Sadly, as Faustina makes clear, sometimes souls have become so hardened that, in spite of all God's efforts, they consciously choose Hell (see *Diary*, 1698). But other times, even though there may not be any external evidence of conversion, the soul accepts this final offer of mercy:

> Outwardly, it seems as if everything were lost, but it is not so. The soul, illumined by a ray of God's powerful final grace, turns to God in the last moment ... while outwardly it shows no sign either of repentance or of contrition.
>
> *Diary*, 1698

It's never too late to pray!

$\mathcal{S}$ECRET 7

The Goal Is Transfiguration

*All of us, gazing with unveiled face
on the glory of the Lord, are being
transformed into the same image
from glory to glory.*

2 Cor 3:18, NAB

A few years ago, a young man went to see my spiritual director, Fr. George Kosicki, who had recently been transferred to a nursing facility for the elderly because of his failing health.

The man had been deeply touched by the Divine Mercy message and devotion and had recently spent a year living on the streets to minister to the homeless. He had been trying to get to the heart of Divine Mercy, the core message and goal of it all.

He had never met Fr. Kosicki, but had heard that he was one of the foremost authorities on Divine Mercy; and Fr. Kosicki's name had repeatedly come to him in prayer, as if the Lord was telling him to go see him.

Fr. Kosicki agreed to see him, but seemed weak and distracted, so he said, "Father, I won't take up much of your time. I just have one question: What's Divine Mercy all about?"

Without any hesitation at all, Fr. Kosicki replied, "Transfiguration."

Full Circle

As I started writing today, an old gag line (one of those "smile but get the message" jokes) popped into my head: "If you don't know where you're going, you're liable to end up somewhere else."

Sometimes, in order to know where you're going, it helps to look back and see where you've been. Everything we've seen so far has been leading up to this chapter, so before going any further, let's take a look at where we've been — the essential realities we've seen through each "secret."

Foreword. More than anything else, *devotion to Divine Mercy* means putting mercy into action, living lives "shaped by mercy" (Pope Francis, Homily, July 7, 2014).

Secret 1. The *Father's plan of mercy* is to introduce each of His children into the Trinity — *to divinize us* and unite us with Him and with each other in mutual self-giving love.

Secret 2. The prerequisite for our participation in this plan is *holiness* — which is only possible if we allow God to fill us with *His* holiness.

Secret 3. The *Divine Mercy Image* shows us "the face of the Father's mercy" (*Face of Mercy*, #1). In this Image we "see" the entire Trinity, the entire plan of God, the entire story of God's creation and re-creation, the entire mystery of Divine Mercy.

Secret 4. God doesn't merely love *more* than we do. He loves *differently*. His mercy is not reserved for the deserving. He doesn't keep a tally sheet and measure out differing degrees of mercy based on behavior.

Secret 5. God is the *Prodigal Father*, freely pouring His mercy out upon all. He is eternally merciful, longing to bless His children and restore them to the fullness of joy.

Secret 6. Everything, everything, everything comes from the Cross through *the Eternal Now*. All the graces of the Father's mercy are endlessly pouring out through the pierced Heart of Jesus and are available to us at each moment of our lives — especially through meditation on the Passion of Christ and worthy reception of the Sacraments of Reconciliation and Eucharist.

And now, here we are at Secret 7. Full circle. Back to God's plan of mercy, His plan of divinization. The process through which we become divinized

— sharing in God's own life, filled with Christ's holiness, living and loving like Him so we can enter into the Trinity Itself — is *transfiguration.*

More specifically, as Pope Benedict XVI refers to it, it's a process of *"progressive transfiguration."* But we'll see more about this later.

An Explosive Process

Sometimes, when I'm giving a talk about this, I start with a little acronym to help people remember what I'm going to be talking about: TNT — Transparency, New Life, and Transfiguration.

Moses goes up a mountain, taking three others with him: Aaron, Nadab, and Abihu. A cloud of glory covers the mountain, and the Lord speaks to him from the cloud.

When Moses comes down from the mountain, there's something radically new and different about him. His face is shining so intensely that the people are afraid to go near him, so he covers his face with a veil. Whenever he enters the Meeting Tent, he removes the veil and converses with God face-to-face. Then he puts it on again before returning to the people (see Ex 24: 1-2, 15-18; 34: 29-35).

Moses has become transparent to God. When the people look at his face, it's as if they're looking through a window — and what they see is the glory of God.

Flash forward. Christ (the new Moses) goes up a mountain, taking three others with him: Peter, James, and John. Suddenly, He is "transfigured before them" (Mt 17:2), and His face shines like the sun. Moses shows up with Elijah, and they converse with Jesus. A bright cloud overshadows them, and the Father's voice proclaims from the cloud, "This is my beloved Son, with whom I am well pleased; listen to him." The three disciples fall on their faces, "filled with awe" (Mt 17:5-6). As John later recounts, they beheld His glory, "glory as of the only-begotten Son" (Jn 1:14).

From Glory to Glory

Glory. Another often-used Christian word. What *is* glory? What is it that they see?

St. Paul speaks of "the glory of Christ, who is the *likeness* of God," and again, of "the glory of God in the *face* of Christ" (2 Cor 4:4, 6; emphasis added). So glory somehow involves being in the likeness of God. And that likeness can be reflected in the human body.

Ring any bells? There are some pretty clear echoes here of some of the *Catechism's* teachings we saw back in Secret 2. Our human bodies are created in such a way — in His image and likeness — that they can *reflect the divine form*. But then, "disfigured by sin" we are "deprived 'of the glory of God,' of his 'likeness.'" So Christ is sent to "assume that 'image' and restore it in the Father's 'likeness.'" How? "By giving it again its Glory, the Spirit who is 'the giver of life'" (#705).

So, the glory of God is manifested in us by His Holy Spirit, the radiating, transforming, life-giving Spirit of God.

What did the people see in Moses' face? What did the disciples see in Christ's face? They saw the manifestation of divinity, the reflected glory of God. Moses and Christ were transfigured, meaning that they radiated God's glory. They had become transparent to God, and divinity was visible in their human bodies.

Fix Your Gaze

That's the goal of Divine Mercy, for each of us to become transparent to God, so restored in the Father's likeness, so filled with God's own life, His holiness, that we reflect His eternal glory.

Take the Divine Mercy Image, for example. St. Faustina didn't see a vision of a *painting*. She saw *Jesus, Himself*, the visible "image of the invisible God" (Col 1:15). (And whenever she looked at the painting, she saw beyond it to the real Image.) Like the disciples at the Transfiguration, she beheld "the glory of God" (*Diary*, 1789).

She writes:

> I kept my gaze fixed upon the Lord; my soul was struck with awe, but also with great joy.
>
> *Diary*, 47

After this, Jesus speaks to her, but not immediately. He allows her to be in awe for a while, simply gazing at Him.

Want to know how to use the Divine Mercy Image

most effectively? *Look* at it. *Gaze* at it. Keep your gaze fixed upon the Lord until you are struck with awe and joy, contemplating the incredible goodness of God, who is always loving you, always blessing you, always inviting you into His Heart.

Become What You Behold

St. Paul records the process of transformation that takes place through this contemplative gazing on the Lord:

> All of us, gazing with unveiled face
> on the glory of the Lord, are being
> transformed into the same image
> from glory to glory.
>
> 2 Cor 3:18, NAB

As we gaze upon the Image, contemplating God's great mercy, *we come to see who God really is and who we are called to be.* Moment by moment, through the grace of God, we are transformed into the image and likeness of what we see, from one degree of glory to the next. We *become what we behold* until we, ourselves, are living reflections of God.

We're not supposed to just hang this Image on a wall; *we're supposed to become it.* The Divine Mercy Image must become our "mountaintop experience," our reminder that Jesus is Mercy Incarnate and that we are each called to become like Him, *transfigured into living images of Divine Mercy,* reflecting and radiating the Father's mercy in the world:

> The vocation of humanity is to *show forth the image of God and to be transformed into the image* of the Father's only Son, ... to make God manifest by acting in conformity with his creation "in the image and likeness of God."
>
> *Catechism,* #1877, 2085; emphasis added

Our vocation is to make God visible *by the way we live,* acting in conformity to the way we were created — in His image and likeness.

I've got to start acting like someone made in the image and likeness of God! I've got to start acting the way He acts, seeing you the way He sees you, loving you the way He loves you. I've got to start seeing God in you and responding to you with a blessing.

Mirror, Mirror on the Wall

The Divine Mercy Image is what you and I should see every time we look in the mirror. *It's an examination of conscience.* Am I a mirror reflection of Christ? Am I transparent to Him so that when people see me they see Him? Do I reflect His tenderness, His gentleness, His patience, His loving gaze from the Cross?

When I look in the mirror, do I see someone with one hand always blessing, the other always inviting everyone into my heart? Do I see the Prodigal Father squandering love, pouring mercy out upon everyone without exception? Do I see someone in whom others can place their trust?

I need to make Faustina's prayer my own:

> I want to be *completely transformed* into Your mercy and *to be Your living reflection*, O Lord. ...
>
> *Diary,* 163

> I expose my heart to the action of Your grace like a crystal exposed to the rays of the sun. *May Your image be reflected in it,* O my

God, to the extent that it is possible to be reflected in the heart of a creature. *Let Your divinity radiate through me.*

Diary, 1336

The One True Image

Earlier I mentioned St. Basil's teaching that "the honor rendered to an image passes to its prototype," so "whoever venerates an image venerates the person portrayed in it." So, as we gaze on the painting that represents Christ, what we're trying to do is connect with Him, to become like Him, *the real Divine Mercy Image.*

Where is the *real* Divine Mercy Image? In Heaven? Yes, of course. But sometimes Heaven can seem pretty far away. Is The Divine Mercy Image anywhere else in a more tangible way, a more "right here and now" way?

Yes. *The Eucharist.* Jesus, in Person — Divine Mercy, Himself— is right here in our midst, in every tabernacle in the world, twenty-four seven.

There's a "veil" over the Eucharist. We look and try to believe what we've been taught, but we're seeing what looks like bread, what looks like wine. If we could lift the veil, what we would see is Jesus as He is portrayed in the Divine Mercy Image.

Every time you receive the Eucharist or spend time in Eucharistic Adoration, see that Image. Because He is truly there. Not the picture, but the prototype — the one that the picture is trying to represent to us. The one true Divine Mercy Image, Jesus Christ.

Jesus Himself, in His full humanity and full divinity, is present for us in the Eucharist. His hand is raised in blessing, He's inviting us into His Eucharistic Heart, and He's pouring out His very life into us all the time. That's the value of Communion and Adoration: to receive that outpouring fountain of love, allowing Jesus — "the radiance of God's glory and the exact representation of his being" (Heb 1:3 NIV) — to radiate *us* to glory.

A Mode of Being

I want to remind you of two things I mentioned before. In Secret 2, I explained that the main way

Christ shares His holiness with us is by *re-creating* us through the sacraments. And earlier, when we were talking about God's plan of divinization, I mentioned Pope Benedict's explanation that eternal life is "not just endless time," but *a whole new way of living* — it's the way God lives.

Those two things are connected. God re-creates us through the sacraments by giving us a new way of living. As Pope John Paul II writes,

> Those who feed on Christ in the Eucharist need not wait until the hereafter to receive eternal life: *they already possess it.*
>
> *The Church of the Eucharist,* #18; emphasis original

And Pope Benedict XVI adds,

> "Eternal life" begins in us even now, thanks to the transformation effected in us by the gift of the Eucharist: ... an innate power making it the principle of new life within us. ... By receiving the body and blood of Jesus Christ we become sharers in the divine life.
>
> *The Sacrament of Charity,* #70

Pope John Paul II defines the Eucharist as "a mode of being," a way of living that passes from Jesus into each of us and is meant to pass through us to others. But in order for us to be able to pass on this way of living, we ourselves first have to "assimilate" Christ's values, Christ's attitudes, Christ's whole way of existing (*Stay With Us Lord*, #25).

Assimilate. To "take in, to gradually absorb so as to become part of."

Pope Benedict uses the same term:

> This act of "eating," is actually a meeting between two persons; it is to allow myself to be penetrated by the life of the One who is Lord. ... The purpose of this communion is the *assimilation* of my life with His, my transformation and configuration with the One who is living Love.
>
> Homily, May 30, 2005

It's as if Christ, in the Eucharist, is saying to you and me:

> *"Here's my way of living, my way of being, my thoughts, my feelings, my attitudes, my values, my perceptions, my way of seeing the*

*world, my way of loving. Take it all into your-
self and then pass it on to others."*

Just as, by gazing at the Divine Mercy Image, we're supposed to become what we behold, so, as we receive the Eucharist (the *real* Divine Mercy Image), we are supposed to *become who we receive*, to become *living Eucharist, living images of Divine Mercy* in the world.

Progressive Transfiguration

This transformation doesn't happen with one reception of the Eucharist; it's a *process*. The more we long for this complete union with Christ, and for what Pope Benedict often calls the "radical newness" that's being offered to us, the more we are able to "take on" Christ's whole way of being and allow it to permeate our entire life (see *The Sacrament of Charity*, #71-84).

Gradually, through each prayerful reception of Communion, each moment spent in Eucharistic Adoration, we become more and more like Christ.

"The Eucharist," Pope Benedict explains, "makes possible, day by day, the *progressive transfiguration* of all those called by grace *to reflect the image* of the Son of God" (*The Sacrament of Charity*, #71).

A Gift to Be Given

It's important to become more and more aware of the "pass it on" requirement that Pope John Paul II emphasized. When Christ passes His "mode of being" on to us through the Eucharist, we are expected to pass it on to others.

The gift of transfiguration is not given as a personal possession for me to cling to and keep for myself. It's a gift to be given, a gift to be shared with others.

Remember the dual nature of the plan of mercy we saw in Secret 1? God doesn't just want to unite *me with Him* in the Trinity; he wants me there *in complete union with His other children* ("Father, that they may be one ..." Jn 17:11).

Pope Benedict and Pope Francis both emphasize this same requirement. Pope Benedict writes,

> The love that we celebrate in the sacrament is not something we can keep to

ourselves. ... *It demands to be shared with all.* What the world needs is God's love; it needs to encounter Christ and to believe in him. ... Nothing is more beautiful than to know Christ *and make him known to others.*

The Sacrament of Charity, #84

Pope Francis has made this the recurrent theme of his whole pontificate — to come out of ourselves, go beyond our comfort zones, and reach out to others:

Jesus speaks in silence in the Mystery of the Eucharist. ... Following him means going out of ourselves and *not making our life a possession of our own,* but rather *a gift to him and to others.* ...

How do I live the Eucharist? ... Do I let myself be transformed by him? Do I let the Lord ... guide me to *going out ever more* from my little enclosure, in order *to give, to share, to love him and others?*

Homily, May 30, 2013

The Transfiguration of the World

So, the goal is not just to be transfigured ourselves,

but to help others to also be transfigured — and not just a few others. We are called to live a completely Eucharistic spirituality, to share in Christ's mission to transform and transfigure the world.

Pope Benedict XVI, in his encyclical, *The Sacrament of Charity*, writes that the transformation of the bread and wine into Christ's body and blood is "meant to set off a process which transforms reality, a process *leading ultimately to the transfiguration of the entire world*" (#11).

And Pope John Paul II makes it clear that we are all to be involved in this process, explaining that all those "who take part in the Eucharist [must] be committed to changing their lives and making them *completely 'Eucharistic'* ... [the] fruit of *a transfigured existence* and a commitment to transforming the world" (*The Church of the Eucharist*, #20).

Back to TNT

A commitment to *transforming the world*. The Eucharist is a gift demanding a *response* — a gift that empowers us and challenges us to become *transparent* to God, filled with the *new life* (Christ's own life) that flows from this "fountain of mercy," and *transfigured* from one degree of glory to another until we become living images of mercy. When enough of us say "yes" to this, the world itself will be transfigured, reflecting the glory of its Creator.

The Mother of Divine Mercy

It seems appropriate to close this chapter with Mary. She is the best example of how to respond to this gift, and she mirrors for us the inseparable relationship we've just seen between Divine Mercy and the Eucharist.

Pope John Paul II calls Mary the "Mother of Divine Mercy," explaining that she received mercy — and *shares in the revelation of mercy* — in a way that "no other person has." She is "the one who has the deepest knowledge" of God's mercy (*Rich in Mercy,* #9).

He also calls her the "Woman of the Eucharist." He explains that, because of her own "profound relationship" with the Eucharist, she is "our teacher in contemplating Christ's face," and she can "guide us towards this most holy sacrament," showing us how to be "conformed to Christ." She is present at each Eucharistic celebration, and is "inseparably united" with the Eucharist (*The Church of the Eucharist*, #53, 57).

The *Catechism* refers to Mary as "wholly transparent" to God (#2674). She was so united to Christ that she became completely transparent to Him. Well, is it any wonder? She carried Him in her womb for nine months. Jesus, the God-Man, Divine Mercy incarnate, *lived exclusively in her* for nine months!

Chosen from all eternity to be the Mother of the Messiah, the Mother of Mercy, Mary was conceived without sin, blessed by the Father "more than any other created person," and adorned with "the 'splendor of an entirely unique holiness'" (*Catechism*, #492).

> Mary ... is the daughter of Zion in person, the ark of the covenant, *the place where the glory of the Lord dwells.* She is "the dwelling of God ... with men." Full of grace, Mary is wholly given over to him who has come to dwell in her.
>
> #2676; emphasis added

In his encyclical, *God Is Love,* Pope Benedict XVI writes that Mary is the "mirror of all holiness," and that magnifying the Lord is "her whole program of life." She is "a woman of faith," because her thoughts are "attuned to the thoughts of God" and "her will is one with the will of God." She "thinks with God's thoughts and wills with God's will" (#41). She *assimilates* Christ's whole way of living.

Sound familiar? Mary is the embodiment of everything I've been talking about. *She shows us who we are supposed to become.* She "shows us what love is, … a pure love which is *not self-seeking*" (#42).

Abandoning herself completely to God, Mary "became a wellspring of the goodness which flows forth from him." If we allow her to lead us to Him, "we too can become capable of true love and *be fountains of living water in the midst of a thirsting world*" (#42).

Overshadowed

To illustrate further what all this means to us, let's take a look at Mary as a teenager. An angel appears to her with a rather amazing announcement: she will conceive, bear a son, and call Him Jesus (which in Hebrew means "God saves"). He's going to be great; He'll be called the Son of the Most High; He'll be given the throne of David; He's going to reign forever; and His kingdom will never end (See Lk 1:26-33).

Wow! Think about that for a minute. If you were a teenage girl, how would you respond to that? Mary simply asks how this is all going to happen, since she has taken a vow of virginity. The angel replies:

> The Holy Spirit will come upon you, and the power of the Most High will overshadow you.
>
> Lk 1:35

The word *overshadow* is very significant here. Remember the cloud that covered the mountain when God spoke to Moses? And the cloud that overshadowed the disciples when Christ was transfigured? Both call to mind the cloud that covered the Meeting Tent in the desert during the Exodus of the Israelites:

> Then the cloud covered the tent of meeting, and the glory of the LORD filled the tabernacle.
>
> Ex 40:34

It's Greek to Me

The word *overshadow* used by the angel to Mary is the same root word used in the ancient Greek version of the Old Testament passage quoted above, describing how the glory of God "overshadowed" the tabernacle, thus making it His dwelling place.

This young girl is being told that, if she says "yes," she will become the new tabernacle, filled with glory, the new dwelling place of God.

As a sign that nothing is impossible for God, the angel then adds that Mary's cousin Elizabeth who was thought to be barren is six months pregnant.

Mary responds with the *Fiat* that changed the world: "Let it be [done] to me according to your word" (Lk 1:38). And at those words of faithfulness and trust, the Son of God took flesh in her womb.

Okay. It's over. The angel has left. Now what? What does Mary do? She's just found out that, of all the women in the history of the world, she's the one chosen to be the Mother of God. So naturally, she does what any other teenage girl would do:

She runs up to a mirror and says, "Wow! It's me! I'm the one! I'm the promised virgin. I'm the fulfillment of all the prophecies!" She grabs her cell phone and calls a friend: "Hey, guess what? You know that promised virgin who's going to bear the Messiah? Well, it's me!"

Pretty ridiculous, huh? But wouldn't that be normal? What would you do if you had just received the greatest honor ever given to anyone? Wouldn't you want to revel in that a little bit? Wouldn't you want to brag a little? Or at least share your amazement?

Mary doesn't do that. No inward turning. No self-focus. What *does* she do? Scripture tells us that she goes "in haste" to help Elizabeth (see Lk 1:39). Her first thought is for someone else. *Her first act is an act of mercy.*

From Fiat to Amen

The Annunciation is Mary's first Holy Communion. She was the first one asked to believe that God Himself wanted to take flesh in her; and by her *Fiat* she became the first living tabernacle.

As St. Faustina expresses it, Mary's heart was "the first tabernacle on earth" (*Diary,* 161):

> You have indeed prepared a tabernacle for Yourself: the Blessed Virgin. Her Immaculate Womb is Your dwelling place, and the inconceivable miracle of Your mercy takes place, O Lord. The Word becomes flesh; God dwells among us, the Word of God, Mercy Incarnate.
>
> *Diary,* 1745

So, bearing Divine Mercy within her, Mary goes in haste to bring Him to Elizabeth. Her Visitation is the first Eucharistic procession in history. Having become a living tabernacle, Mary now becomes a living monstrance, so transparent to God, so united with Him that His Divine Presence radiates from every part of her being. Having received the fullness of mercy, she now becomes a bearer of mercy.

I wish we knew if she met anybody along the way and, if so, how she affected them. Unfortunately, Scripture doesn't tell us anything about her journey. But we know what happened when she got to Elizabeth's house:

When she arrived, she hollered, "Elizabeth!
It's Mary!" Elizabeth cried out, "Mary! It's so
good to see you! Thanks for coming!"

I know. I lied again. But wouldn't that have been
normal? Elizabeth probably didn't know Mary was
coming. Wouldn't she have been surprised and
delighted to see her?

Elizabeth's actual response is off the charts:

She exclaimed with a loud cry, "Blessed
are you among women, and blessed is the
fruit of your womb!"

Lk 1:42

Not exactly the way you'd expect your cousin to
greet you. I can imagine a modern-day Mary replying,

"Hey, Elizabeth, chill out! It's just me, Mary."

But, of course, Mary didn't say that, and Elizabeth
continues her emotional response:

Who am I, that the Mother of my Lord
should come to me? For at the sound of
your greeting, the babe in my womb leaped

for joy. Blessed are you for believing that the
Lord's words to you would be fulfilled.

Paraphrase of Lk 1:43-45

Elizabeth is in awe! And she seems to know
everything that has happened. How does she know
all this? There are no cell phones. No overnight mail.
And yet Elizabeth responds to Mary's greeting with
complete knowledge, reverence, and faith. What's
that all about?

St. Luke already told us a few lines earlier:

When Elizabeth heard the greeting of
Mary, the child leaped in her womb; and
Elizabeth was filled with the Holy Spirit.

Lk 1:41, RSV-CE

When Elizabeth heard the *greeting*? The sound of
Mary's greeting — her *voice* — caused Elizabeth to
be so completely filled with the Holy Spirit that she
received a full, prophetic "word of knowledge" about
the Annunciation and was able to respond with complete faith that her cousin was now the Mother of
God. The *sound* of Mary's voice caused John the
Baptist to be baptized in his mother's womb.

That's transparency! She was so filled with God, so one with Him, that *He was even in her voice.* The Father had "found the dwelling place where his Son and his Spirit could dwell among men" (*Catechism*, #721). And from that dwelling place, He could now pour His mercy out — through her voice, her eyes, her face, her whole being.

This is the effect of one person transparent to God; one person whose life is a complete "yes" to God; one person who receives and adores; one person who becomes living Eucharist.

You and I are called to echo that "yes" and that adoration every time we go to receive Communion. Pope John Paul II says that there is "a profound analogy" between the *Fiat* that Mary said at the Annunciation and the "Amen" that you and I say when we receive the Eucharist (see *The Church of the Eucharist*, #55).

So, the next time you go to receive and the priest says, "The Body of Christ," hear him asking,

> *"Do you believe that God Himself, wants to take flesh in you? Wants to live in you? Wants*

*to pass His whole way of living into you? Do
you believe this, and will you say 'yes' to it?"*

As you say "Amen," let your "Amen" be a *Fiat*.

Yes, Lord. Let it be done to me according to Your word. Yes, Lord, take flesh in
me. Let me become living Eucharist, a living image of Your mercy. Let me, like Mary,
bring You within me everywhere I go.

Let me be a living monstrance, so that in
my eyes, in my voice, in my whole being,
people will see Your truth, Your beauty, Your
tenderness, Your compassion, Your
patience, Your forgiveness. Lord, let me *be*
Your mercy in the world.

AFTERWORD

"Even More!"

*Even when you feel discouraged or
weighed down by personal failures or sin,
trust even more in the love of God for you.
Turn to him for mercy, forgiveness, and love.*

Pope John Paul II

Okay, decision time. We know who God is, and
we've seen His plan. We've seen how Our Lady
stepped wholeheartedly into that plan with a
resounding "yes" that shook the world. So, what
about you? Who are you going to be? How are you

going to respond? How complete will your "yes" be?

You may have noticed the dedication to Fr. George Kosicki in the front of this book. I have never met anyone more "steeped in mercy." As I wrote in the dedication, he was a man "for whom Divine Mercy was a way of life."

But he was never "done," never content with being "good enough," but always trying to go deeper in his relationship with God, always asking for the grace to say a more complete "yes" and be transformed into a living image of mercy.

I remember the day he told me that he was now beginning each morning with a simple question: "Father, what can I do to please you today?" And, over and over, he heard the same answer in his heart:

> To please me, be *present* to me, with your heart in the heart of Mary — trusting, rejoicing, and giving thanks.

I never met a man so joyful, so excited about "the things of God." Every day he would share some new insight he had received in Adoration, some new thought or awareness of how to live Divine Mercy.

Only One Commandment

Fr. Kosicki realized that, in reality, there's only one commandment: love — love of God and love of neighbor. And he knew that *neighbor* meant everyone.

Like St. Faustina, whom he called his "sister," he had come to understand and take into himself the great desire of Christ, the great thirst of Christ revealed in His cry from the Cross. And with Faustina, he tried to fulfill, more and more, the Lord's plea to her that we saw earlier:

> **I thirst. I thirst for the salvation of souls. Help Me ... to save souls. Join your sufferings to My Passion and offer them to the heavenly Father for sinners.**
>
> *Diary*, 1032

"All for souls" became Fr. Kosicki's daily response to every annoyance, every difficulty, every inconvenience, every disruption to his plans, every suffering. He was constantly encouraging me to place all my misery in the mercy of God, offering it out of love for others. And he often reminded me that when we offer Christ all our "misery" — whatever inevitable sufferings we experience — for the sake of others, He not only pours His mercy out on *them*, but fills *us* more as well.

Mercy-full and Mercy-flow

Another Christian spelling lesson. Next time you spell *merciful*, think it as mercy-full. Fr. Kosicki wrote and taught extensively that we can't really be merciful to others until we're *full* of mercy ourselves. He saw God's love as a "constantly flowing, creative power." The Father's love, eternally flowing *to Jesus*, flows *through Jesus* to us as mercy. We are called to tap into that *flow of mercy*, receiving it and letting it flow through *us*.

Trust *opens us to receive* all that God wants to give us, so the more we trust, the more God's mercy flows into us and overflows from us to others. Fr. Kosicki's favorite quote was Christ's "mercy-flow" promise to St. Faustina:

> **When a soul approaches me with trust,**
> **I fill it with such an abundance of graces**

**that it cannot contain them within itself,
but radiates them to other souls.**

Diary, 1074

I never really understood — in my gut — what this overflowing of mercy is really all about until I read Pope Benedict's explanation of the Parable of the Good Samaritan (see Lk 10:25-37). I knew that the call to be merciful involved having compassion on others, but I didn't really know what that meant.

A man, robbed and beaten, lies helpless on the side of the road. Unlike the priest and the Levite, who see him, but pass by on the other side of the road, the Samaritan has compassion on him, binds up his wounds, and takes care of him.

Pope Benedict writes that today's translations of this passage are not true to the original. To say that he has "compassion" is not strong enough. What really happens is that *"his heart is wrenched open"* so completely that he is *compelled* to do whatever he can to alleviate the wounded man's suffering.

Like Jesus on the Cross, whose Heart was torn open by the lance, we are each called to let our hearts be "wrenched open" by the suffering we see around us, to come out of ourselves and reach out to others.

Trust Even More!

Convinced that everything comes through trust and that we need to trust more completely so that we can love and reach out to others more completely, Fr. Kosicki did everything he could to remind himself of this, relying on the Lord's great promise to St. Faustina:

> The graces of My mercy are drawn by means of one vessel only, and that is — trust. The more a soul trusts, the more it will receive.
>
> *Diary,* 1578

Remember the "Covenant of Mercy" we saw in Secret 3? As a fruit of that covenant relationship, Christ allows us to determine how much grace He gives. He speaks about this so strongly to St. Faustina that it boggles the mind:

> I am making Myself *dependent* upon

your trust: if your trust is great, then My generosity will be without limit. ...

Your great trust in Me *forces* Me to continuously grant you graces.

Diary, 548, 718

Fr. Kosicki's "battle cry" became "Trust even more!" This was the message he preached most often and offered constantly in spiritual direction. Every room of his hermitage was filled with visual reminders to trust — little 3x5 cards, on which he had scrawled, "Trust even more!"

They were everywhere: little signs on the bathroom mirror, over the kitchen sink, on the stove, under every light switch and every picture — any place where he would be most likely to notice and remember: "Trust even more!"

It's important to keep in mind the reason for all this emphasis on trust. Trust is the key that unlocks the door of mercy. We are called to *receive* His mercy and let it *radiate* through us; and the more we trust, the more we can do that. Being merciful doesn't just mean doing nice things for people. Social work, social justice, is not enough if it's not motivated and fueled by union with God. We're called to be merciful *as our heavenly Father is merciful*, trusting in Him to fill us with *His way of loving* so we can pass it on.

Back to the beginning. It's decision time. Time for a fuller answer to the essential question. The question set before Adam and Eve, the question offered to Mary, the question answered by Christ three times in the Garden, the question that awaits us at every moment of choice: "Whom shall you serve?"

Let us answer again and again, "As for me and my house, we will serve the LORD" (Jos 24:15).

Pope Francis has a favorite phrase: "Let us ask ourselves ... ." So, let's do that. How am I serving the Lord's plan of mercy? How am I helping Him in His thirst for souls? Am I trying to trust even more? To love as Jesus loves? To forgive as He forgives?

Am I asking Him to fill me so full of mercy that I can radiate it to others? Am I allowing my heart to be so *wrenched open* by the woundedness of those around me that I'm *compelled* to try to help them?

Can I say with Jesus, "The very inner depths of My being are filled to overflowing with mercy, and it is being poured out upon all" (*Diary*, 1784)?

I encourage you to continue asking yourself these questions, and I offer you this Communion meditation by my daughter Erin. It has become a great reminder to me of what Divine Mercy is all about.

Overflow

What use is it if I receive You
and do not bear You to the world?
"Mary went in haste ..."
What use is it if I join myself to You in love and do not love my brother?
"They'll know you are my disciples ..."
Is it even possible to be truly united to Goodness and not share that goodness?
What kind of union is it, if I stay my same self thereafter?
Do not allow me to remain as I am, Jesus.
Help me to prepare my heart for true union with You,
A union that will reveal You to the world uniquely through me.
For what use is it if You come to me and I refuse You to my neighbor?
What use is it, Lord, if You fill me and I do not overflow?

© Erin Flynn

Notes, Sources, and References

FOREWORD
Monopoly® Spirituality

Page 3: "Mercy is the very foundation …" Pope Francis, *Face of Mercy, Bull of Indiction of the Extraordinary Jubilee of Mercy*, #10, 2.

Page 11: "We are called …" Pope Francis, Homily, July 7, 2014.

SECRET 1
God Has a Plan

Page 13: "God has given …" *The Liturgy of the Hours*, Vol. IV (New York: Catholic Book Publishing, 1976), p. 683.

Page 17: "God in his deepest mystery …" Pope John Paul II, as cited in *Puebla* (Boston: Daughters of St. Paul, 1979), p. 86.

Page 17: "Such is the …" see Eph 1:4-5, 9; Rom 8:15, 29.

Page 20: "In the beginning …" *The Liturgy of the Hours*, Vol. II (New York: Catholic Book Publishing, 1976), p. 17. St. Irenaeus, *Against Heresies*, VI, 14, 1.

Page 23: "He was begotten …" Council of Chalcedon (451): DS 301; cf. Heb 4:15.

Page 26: "come to share in …" Roman Missal, 24.

Page 26: "By the participation …" St. Athanasius, *Ep. Serap.* 1, 24: PG 26, 585 and 588.

Page 27: "The only begotten …" St. Thomas Aquinas, *Opusc.* 57: 1-4.

Page 28: "Eternity is not just …" *God Is Near Us*, (San Francisco: Ignatius Press, 2003), p. 137.

Page 34: "We are not some casual …" Pope Benedict XVI, Homily, April 26, 2005.

Page 39: "God has given us …" Ephesians 1:3-10. Translation from *The Mundelein Psalter* (Archdiocese of Chicago: Liturgy Training Publications, 2007).

Page 44: "The Father is wholly …" Council of Florence (1442): DS 1331.

SECRET 2
Good Enough Isn't Good Enough

Page 47: "To be a saint …" Homily, February 23, 2014.

Page 52: "All Christians …" *Lumen Gentium*, #40.

Page 57: "God fashioned …" St. Irenaeus, *Dem ap.* 11:SCh 62, 48-49 "like us in all …" Heb 4:15.

Page 58: "Disfigured by sin …" Rom 3:23.

Page 59: "The Son himself …" Cf. Jn 1:14; Phil 2:7.

Page 59: "It is in Christ …" Col 1:15; cf. 2 Cor 4:4, and Cf. GS 22.

Page 60: "to respond to …" Cf. Jn 1:12-18; 17:3; Rom 8:14-17; 2 Pet 1:3-4.

Page 63: "Holiness is what I …" *Holiness*, Micah Stampley, © 2005.

SECRET 3
It's Not Just a Picture of Jesus

Page 65: "Mercy has become living …" *Face of Mercy* #1, April 11, 2015.

Page 68: "Faustina felt such an obligation …" Fr. Seraphim Michalenko, MIC, "*The Sacred Image of The Divine Mercy*," Conference in Stockbridge, MA, 1991.

Page 71: "the honor …" St. Basil, *De Spiritu Sancto*, 45, p. 32, 149C.

Page 77: "Christ is, in person …" Vatican City, May 26, 2005, Corpus Christi Procession.

Page 83: "drawing open the garment …" Letter from Fr. Michael Sopocko to Fr. Julian Chrosciechowsi, MIC, 1958.

Page 84: "says, 'Come to Me.'…" *Mother Teresa, A Life for God: The Mother Teresa Reader*, compiled by LaVonne Neff (Ann Arbor, MI: Servant Publications, 1995), p. 180.

Page 90: "turning of God …" *Sacrament of Charity*, #9.

Page 93: "Behold this Heart …" Jesus to St. Margaret Mary Alacoque, as cited by Robert A. Stackpole, STD, *Divine Mercy: A Guide from Genesis to Benedict XVI* (Stockbridge, MA: Marian Press, 2008), p. 153.

Page 94: "How often …" Jesus to Sr. Josepha Menendez, *Ibid.*, p. 155.

Page 97: "Now, anytime …" Vinny Flynn, *21 Ways to Worship: A Guide to Eucharistic Adoration* (Stockbridge, MA: MercySong, Inc., 2012), p. 100.

Page 99: "Contractual relations …" Scott Hahn Lecture: "Salvation History: One Holy Family": http://www.star.ucl.ac.uk/~vgg/rc/aplgtc/hahn/m2/slvhst1.html.

Page 105: "entire frontal position..." Letter from Fr. Michael Sopocko to Fr. Julian Chrosciechowsi, MIC, April 1, 1955.

Page 106: "loving and merciful …" Letter from Fr. Michael Sopocko to Fr. Julian Chrosciechowsi, MIC, 1958.

Page 108: "Who is Jorge Mario Bergolio …" Interview with Pope Francis by Antonio Spadaro, S.J., *America Magazine*, September 30, 2013.

Page 108: "Jesus wants me to tell you …" Mother Teresa, Varanasi Letter, March 25, 1993.

SECRET 4
God Loves Backwards

Page 111: "I am more generous …" *Diary*, #1275.

Page 115: "We learn early …" Vinny Flynn, *7 Secrets of Confession* (Stockbridge, MA, 2013), p. 17.

Page 119: "We look at our behavior …" *Ibid.*, p. 18.

Page 125: "He sees everything …" *Ibid.*, p.128.

SECRET 5
Prodigal Doesn't Mean Bad

Page 131: "The very inner depths of My being …" *Diary*, 1784.

SECRET 6
You Should Always Pray Now and Then

Page 153: "Eternal life is there …" *God Is Near Us*, p. 137.

Page 159: "grant unimaginable graces …" Rev. Ignacy Rozycki, *Essential Features of the Devotion to The Divine Mercy* (Stockbridge, MA: Marian Press, 2000), p. 19.

Page 180: "To the satisfaction …" *Ibid.*, pp. 24-25.

Page 184: "…unimaginable Mercy …" *Ibid.*, pp. 20-21.

Page 187: "Sin without repentance is the only obstacle …" Dr. Robert Stackpole, "On Going to Confession Before Mercy Sunday," March 28, 2007: http://www.thedivinemercy.org/news/ On-Going-to-Confession-Before-Mercy-Sunday-2618.

Page 190: "The very depths …" as cited in *The Divine Mercy Message and Devotion*, p. 41.

Page 193: "From the depths …" Pope Francis, *Face of Mercy*, #25.

SECRET 7
The Goal Is Transfiguration

Page 205: "progressive transfiguration …" *Sacrament of Mercy*, p. 71.

Page 207: "deprived of the …" Rom 3:23, and "assume that image…" Cf. Jn 1:14; Phil 2:7.

Page 221: "splendor of …" *LG*, 53, 56.

Page 221: "the dwelling of God …" Rev 21:3.

AFTERWORD
"Even More!"

Page 231: "Even when you feel discouraged …" Pope St. John Paul II, Homily, February 8, 1986.

Page 235: "heart is wrenched …" *Jesus of Nazareth* (New York: Doubleday, 2007), p. 197.

Other Titles
by Vinny Flynn